Improvising Jazz

Jerry Coker

A FIRESIDE BOOK
Published by Simon & Schuster
New York London Toronto Sydney

To my wife
Patty
whose helpful suggestions
and patient proofreading
greatly facilitated the
writing of this book.

First FIRESIDE EDITION, 1987

Published by Simon & Schuster, Inc.
Simon & Schuster Building
Rockefeller Center
1230 Avenue of the Americas
New York, NY 10020

FIRESIDE and colophon are registered trademarks
of Simon & Schuster, Inc.

Manufactured in the United States of America

30 29 28 27 26 25 24 23 22

Library of Congress Cataloging in Publication Data

Coke, Jerry.
   Improvising jazz.

   Reprint. Originally published: Englewood Cliffs,
N.J.: Prentice-Hall, 1964.
   1. Improvisation (Music)   2. Jazz music—
Instruction and study.   I. Title.
MT68.C64   1986   785.42   86-13845
ISBN 0-671-62829-1 Pbk.

Foreword

Since the birth of American Jazz and in its struggle to develop, there has been a great need for both the literature and theory pertaining to the music as contained in this book, IMPROVISING JAZZ. This is certainly a most welcome contribution. I have been through the book in all of its details and find it an excellent treatise on the subject. I am sure both Mr. Coker and the publishers have something in which they can be extremely proud, as the book can serve both as a text book or as a self-teaching device. I am especially delighted to know that IMPROVISING JAZZ is now a reality.

stan kenton

Foreword

The training, care, and feeding of the jazz musician is something about which many of us ought to be more concerned. For jazz is a significant and vital musical language truly of our time, if only because it was born and bred in the twentieth century. And its value has increased with the years as it has developed beyond its relatively humble and isolated beginnings to become a sophisticated art form, which speaks an international, world-wide language.

This book will undoubtedly raise once again the old question of whether jazz can or should be taught. And I suppose many still feel that it should not. In fact, I never cease to be amazed at the tenacity with which various anachronistic attitudes and prejudices regarding jazz persist, despite overwhelming evidence that the face of jazz has undergone some rather radical changes in the last decade or two. In view of these changes, it is surprising that the "teaching" of jazz and the whole question of "formal education" in jazz is a highly controversial issue. Only religion and politics seem to be capable of generating more heated discussions. But then, the vehemence of these discussions in itself attests to how much is at stake, and it indicates much about the vitality of the subject under discussion.

I should like to place the practical aspects of this book in the context of the professional realities which the young jazz musician of today faces. As jazz broadens its expressive and technical scope, it will make increasingly greater demands on its performers and composers. To clarify this assumption graphically, one need only compare the musical knowledge required to play jazz in 1925 with that necessary in 1943 (let alone 1963). In 1925 no self-respecting jazz musician aspired to read or write music, nor did the music of the day demand it. By the same token, today no self-respecting musician could survive without the ability to read and write musical notation—and those few that still exist are quickly trying to remedy such shortcomings.

In bygone days, the young jazz musician acquired his skills (his "bag", in jazz parlance) in those two now-defunct institutions, the "jam session" and the "big band." Here he learned his métier. He gained experience in the practical every-day challenges of creating music. He learned the art of pacing himself, artistically and physically. He learned from his fellow players or from his leader. And above all, he had time to learn by trial and error, to try out new ideas, even at the risk of failing. He had time to edit himself and to acquire the subtle art of artistic discrimination. For the young player of today these opportunities are virtually non-existent. The jam session and big band are a memory of the past. Deprived of these means which represented, in effect, the "educational process" of yesteryear, the young player of today is thrown out in the professional arena and left to fend for himself as best he can. Perhaps the "stage band" development of recent years will help to fill this void. It is still too early to say, but there are signs that this is already a beneficent influence.

In any event, a book such as this one fills the gap left by the demise of the jam session and the road-traveling band. And a book such as this one indicates that jazz has arrived at the stage where it can develop its own teaching and analytical methods, relative to its own special needs and standards.

There are a number of myths which, by their weed-like persistence, contribute much to the controversy surrounding the subject of teaching jazz and its characteristic techniques. One of these is a myth that was borrowed from "classical" music and, in a slightly refurbished form, applied to jazz. This myth consists of the unfortunate notion that the creation of music is a vague, nebulous act fundamentally outside the control of the creator, that is, the composer; and that there is a state called "inspiration" which periodically descends from "above," being granted only to those composers who, for equally nebulous reasons, are especially endowed to receive such inspirations. A corollary of this fantasy is that such ingredients as thought and work (other than the mere notating of the "inspiration" on music paper), in fact any intellectual activity whatever, are anathema to "true" artistic creativity.

In improvised jazz, where even the "work" of notating the music is not by its very nature required, this misconception of the creative process seemed even more readily applicable. Indeed, until quite recently, if one dared to suggest that King Oliver or Charlie Parker did some kind of "thinking" before, during, or after a given solo *about* that solo, one was ostracized as a spoilsport, taking all the fun out of jazz, or at the very least as not very "hip." Solos were thought to emanate full-blown from the mouth and fingers of the player, without benefit of any intermediary such as the brain.

This deception is and was possible because very few people bother to make the distinction between what is conscious and what is subconscious in the creative process. In fact, this point often leads to the further fallacy that, if a composer or improviser did not *consciously* conceive, let us say, a certain rhythmic pattern or an intervallic relationship, then that pattern or relationship did not actually exist in the composer's mind. This fallacy conveniently ignores the fact that a relationship, once it has been discovered and proven to exist, *exists* and is operative as such whether its creator was fully or dimly or perhaps not at all aware of it at the moment of creation.

This seeming paradox is easily explained by the fact that the creative process occurs at all levels of consciousness, ranging from minimal to total awareness. This, in turn, is possible because "inspiration" occurs precisely at that moment when the most complete mental and psychological preparation for a given task (be it only the choice of the next note, for example) has been achieved. Inspiration is like a seed which cannot come forth until the ground has been prepared and a certain formative period has elapsed. In a sense, the composer, when he is "inspired," is *discovering* the next move. But this discovery can occur only when all or almost all of the inherent possibilities for that next move have been appraised. We tend to forget how much in the creative act is negative, i.e. how much of it consists of discarding that which is not relevant or valid, so that by a process of elimination we arrive at that single "discovery" which is (presumably) most valid. This process can take hours or weeks, or—and this is common in the case of improvisors—only fractions of a second.

Thus what I have here called "the most complete mental and psychological preparation" is really the crux of the matter. It is the requisite condition under which inspiration can take wings. And if this is so, obviously some kind or some degree of mental, if you will, "intellectual" process must take place. This may, of course, take many forms, ranging from very specific thinking about a very specific problem to the most comprehensive and elementary kind of preparation, which we call "training" or "study."

In the over-all scheme of preparation, it is at this elementary level that this valuable book takes its position. It is one of a rapidly growing number of books and studies being made available to the jazz student, which reflect the attitude that "education" and "learning" are not necessarily incompatible with the pursuit of jazz, that the "intellect" is a vital and inseparable part of the art of improvising. On this the book takes a refreshingly firm stand.

The implications of this attitude are in themselves of enormous value, especially in so far as they may in time break down the barriers to the teaching of jazz still prevalent in our educational institutions. But this book's value is not only an implicit one. It has a decidedly practical application as well. Indeed this is its primary purpose: to give the beginning jazz improvisor the rudimentary musical-theoretical tools he will need as a professional musician. If it deals with this subject at an elementary level, this is good news; and it does so with a welcome thoroughness that takes nothing for granted, whether it be the name jazz musicians give to a simple chord or the fundamental chord progression of the twelve-bar blues.

The book is obviously the work of a man who has had to deal with these problems both in his own development as a practicing musician of considerable note and as a teacher of wide experience.

gunther schuller

Contents

Introduction

Few methods have been designed for group improvisation, which, in essence, is a spontaneous exchange or interplay of musical ideas and moods. Jazz music, with its roots in basic rhythms and simple melodies, has developed *naturally* into a blend of musicianship, humanity, and intellect, having universal appeal. Improvisation has existed in other styles, but in the classical music of Western civilization its use has been stifled by enlarged instrumentations and the complexity of compositional techniques which have made no allowances for this means of individual expression. The composer achieves the effect of spontaneity when his written music flows naturally and is well played.

Jazz has brought about a renaissance in improvisation, providing a style which is conducive to spontaneous creation by utilizing standard musical elements, such as 4/4 time, songs of uniform length and form (usually 32 measures in length, with an A-A-B-A structure), fairly standardized instrumentation, steady tempi, consistent and logical harmonies, stylized melodies and rhythms, and even an established order of introductions, statements of themes, sequence of soloists, and codas and endings. Such an established framework as we find in jazz improvisation is as useful to the jazz player as the twelve tone system is to the atonalist composer. The characteristics of the style make for swift decisions, enabling the music to move along without interruption. This is not to say that jazz music has always been and will always stay within the aforementioned boundaries dictated by its style, any more than it would be correct to state that twelve tone music is without potential for further development. Jazz has already begun to expand its resources by absorbing the multitude of musical techniques existing in other styles of music. Improvisation in any of the existing styles offers the musician the opportunity to utilize his technical ability to its fullest extent, while enjoying the creative freedom of spontaneous composition. In our present culture, the bulk of the activity in improvisation is in jazz music.

This book is designed to equip you with the understanding of the theoretical principles used in jazz, presented in logical sequence as they apply to the ultimate improvised performance. As a prerequisite to this study, the student must have some technical proficiency and should be reasonably acquainted with major and minor scales.

The absorption and utilization of theory and techniques, which are the improvisor's tools, can in no way guarantee an interesting musical personality. Each jazz player will find his own musical style and his style will be subject to the criticism of the listener. He may develop a style which is physical or cerebral, faddish or original, blatant or subtle, rambling or formful, ugly or beautiful, flexible or inflexible, tense or relaxed, exciting or dull, or any combination of these extremes, all of which could be the product of a technically equipped player. The style of the individual player is affected by his personality, his intelligence, his talent, and his coordination, all of which are beyond the scope of this text.

1

the Improvisor's Basic Tools

Five factors are chiefly responsible for the outcome of the jazz player's improvisation: intuition, intellect, emotion, sense of pitch, and habit. His intuition is responsible for the bulk of his originality; his emotion determines the mood; his intellect helps him to plan the technical problems and, with intuition, to develop the melodic form; his sense of pitch transforms heard or imagined pitches into letter names and fingerings; his playing habits enable his fingers to quickly find certain established pitch patterns. Four of these elements of his thinking—intuition, emotion, sense of pitch, and habit—are largely subconscious. Consequently, any control over his improvisation must originate in the intellect. While the intellect is limited in its capacity for control over intuition and emotion, it can be responsible for the training of the ear and for establishing a variety of helpful finger patterns, in addition to its function of solving technical problems.

It would be difficult to place these five factors into proportionate values. Some improvisors rely more heavily on certain factors; others will depend on other factors. A few gifted players are able to perform adequately by relying completely on the subconscious elements. All but the rare genius, however, are eventually limited in their development. They need special study, due to the problems of deeply ingrained habits, the unaccustomed rigors of working up to every potential, and, in some instances, an inability to admit or evaluate shortcomings. The ability to evaluate is important and will be discussed in Appendix A.

Since the intellect is the only completely controllable factor, we will approach the problem of learning to play jazz almost solely through this factor, and hope that the other four (intuition, emotion, the sense of pitch, and habit) will progress at the rate established by the intellect. If, in the first lessons, the approach seems cold and calculated, remember that most artistic accomplishment requires academic training. This training is the foundation upon which to build, and it will strengthen your capacity to enjoy fully your own work and the work of others.

Let us now look more deeply into the problems of the intellect. The improvisor must know, for his own musical security, the general framework on which he bases his improvisation. This, in most cases, is a song form, either twelve or thirty-two measures in length, which is repeated as many times as necessary so that maximum temporal freedom is allowed to each of the individual improvisors in a jazz ensemble. The player's knowledge of the material must include: (1) the length of the tune; (2) its thematic and harmonic construction, in a general sense (A-B-A, A-A-B-A, etc.), and the length of these sections; (3) the tonality of the tune and any temporary modulations to other keys; (4) the individual chords of the progression and how they are related to one another; (5) the scales which fit the various chords and sections of the tune; and (6) the emotional equality or mood of the tune.

These are by no means the *only* considerations confronting the improvisor. Rather, they comprise the basic minimum of his needed working knowledge of the material. Additional considerations will be discussed after you have grasped the more general techniques for improvising.

Let us examine and analyze, in the light of the previously mentioned aspects, an example of a typical tune used by improvisors, the "blues" tune. (The terms *tune* and *song* are used in a liberal sense here, since the original melody is largely ignored and obscured by the jazz player's improvisations. His creative endeavor is enriched by his own melodies, based on the *chord progressions* of the tunes he uses.) The blues progression shown in Figure 1 is only one of many existing chord progressions to that tune and is an example of one of the more basic and simple patterns.

FIGURE 1

The slanted lines below each chord symbol represent the beats. The first letter of each of the chord symbols indicates the pitch upon which the chord is built, called the *root*. A capital "M" signifies a *major triad* and a small "m" indicates a *minor triad*. A triad is a three-note chord made up of the first, third, and fifth degrees of a scale, a major scale for a major triad and a minor scale for a minor triad. The number "7" indicates that the seventh degree above the root has been added to the triad, transforming it into a *seventh chord*. If the symbol for the seventh contains a capital "M," the chord is constructed from the first, third, fifth, and seventh degrees of a major scale built on the root of the chord. A natural minor scale is used to determine the correct spelling of the first, third, fifth, and seventh scale degrees of a chord having the symbol, "m7." If the symbol includes only the root name and a "7," without the "M" or "m" to indicate whether the chord is major or minor, it is understood that the triad is major, but the seventh is lowered a half-step from its position in the major scale. The written names for these types of seventh chords are:

M7—major seventh chord
m7—minor seventh chord
7—seventh chord or dominant seventh chord

Examples of the construction of these chords would be as follows:

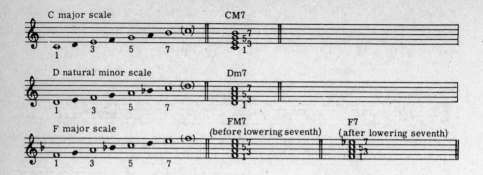

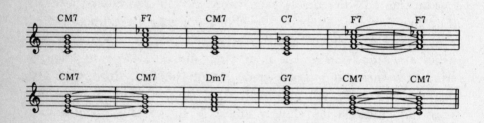

A clearer projection of the harmony of the blues progression of Figure 1 would now be:

In further analyzing the blues, we find the tune to be twelve measures long, and in the key of C major. (For the present, let it suffice to say that we guess it to be in C major because it starts and ends on a C major seventh chord.) Since there is no given melody in Figure 1, we cannot determine the motivic construction; however, notice that the progression seems basically to contain four measures in C, then an implied feeling of F for two measures, followed by six measures of C chords and chords which are closely related to the key of C. These sections might be labeled A-B-A. We will discuss key modulations in a later section, when you have digested the terminology and information needed for such analysis. The term *blues*, in jazz, usually denotes a chord progression twelve bars in length, and also describes its mood.

Since melody ordinarily moves by steps, rather than from one chord tone to another, it would be helpful to decide what notes can be played *between* chord tones. For the major seventh chord we shall use a major scale built on the root of the chord; hence the scale for the CM7 chord would be a C major scale. This gives us the additional notes D, F, and A to act as melodic joiners between the more important melodic notes on C, E, G, and B. For the F7 chord we will use an F scale, but lowering the seventh degree (E) by a half-step to accommodate the E♭ used in the chord.

The Dm7 and G7 chords, as stated earlier, are closely related to the key of C. Therefore a C major scale may be used on these chords, but with the scale beginning on the roots of those chords.

The above scale on D is an example of a scale construction known as the *Dorian Mode* which belongs to a family of modal scales discussed in music theory and music history texts. The scale on G, also shown above, corresponds to the construction of another modal scale from that family, the *Mixolydian Mode*. Hereafter, the scale which uses the same tones as a major scale of a major second (two half-steps) lower will be referred to as the *Dorian Mode*. Similarly, the scale whose root is the fifth degree of a major scale, and which uses the same pitches, will be called the *Mixolydian Mode*.

Figure 2 shows a summation of what we have just learned about the blues progression. This information should be analyzed and studied carefully as preparation for improvisation on the blues progression of Figure 1.

•/. = repeat previous measure.

length: 12 measures
form: A (4 measures)—B (2 measures)—A (6 measures)
mood: "blue"

FIGURE 2

projects

1. Spelling chords:

Write in the chord notes for each of the following symbols.

2. Playing chords:

(a) Play the above chords in two octaves, up and down.

(b) Copy only the symbols from above on a separate sheet of paper
and practice the chords, represented by the symbols, in two octaves,
up and down.

3. Writing scales which accompany chords:

(a) Write a major scale on the roots of all the major seventh chords
in (a) of Number 1 above.

(b) Write a scale beginning on the second degree on the roots of all
the minor seventh chords in (b) of Number 1.

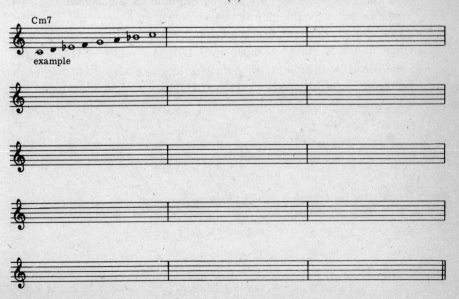

(c) Write a scale beginning on the fifth degree on the roots of all the seventh chords in (c) of Number 1.

4. Playing scales which accompany chords:
   (a) Read the scales you have written in Number 3, playing them in two octaves (think of the chord as you play them).
   (b) Using the symbols you recopied for (b) of Number 2, play the accompanying scales for the chords implied by the symbols in two octaves (think of the chords as you play them).
5. Supply the chord and accompanying scale spellings to the following A-A-B-A chord progression. Use the scale of the second degree on all minor seventh chords and the scale of the fifth degree on all seventh chords.

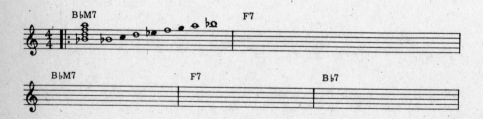

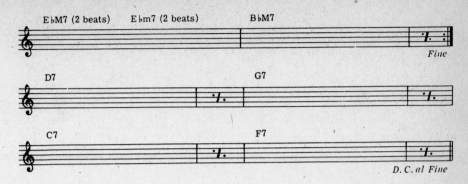

D. C. al Fine

an Introduction to Melody

Melody is (1) one of the essential elements of music, along with harmony and rhythm; (2) that part of music which is heard most prominently; (3) a component of music capable of division into smaller fragments, such as periods, phrases, or motifs; and (4) a group of fragments woven into symmetrical patterns. The *motif* is the smallest melodic entity from which much of the remainder of the music is written or played.

Figure 3 shows a twelve-measure solo on the blues progression,

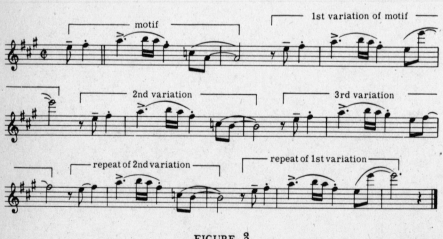

FIGURE 3

having six melodic fragments (in brackets) which occur in a symmetrical pattern. The last five fragments are related by obvious
similarities to the first fragment, which we shall call the *motif*.
Because they vary only slightly from the motif, these five fragments
would be called *variations*. The use of this sort of melodic organi-
zation, often called the *theme* (motif) *and variations* form, seems
to be a natural tendency of both improvisors and composers. Most
music, whether composed spontaneously or not, can be analyzed,
therefore, in terms of motifs and variations of motifs. The degree
to which this type of melodic form exists would of course depend
upon the individual artist's ability and desire to use it.

Some jazz solos are made up of a steady stream of eighth notes,
divided into unrelated phrases by infrequent pauses for breath or
thought. We shall call this type of improvisation a *linear* style. It
is sometimes difficult to analyze in terms of motivic construction,
but we can appreciate it for its continuity, smoothness, contours,
note choices, and placement of rhythmic accents, rather than for
its melodic form. Figure 4 is an example of a solo in the linear style.

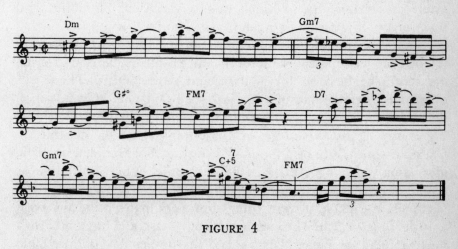

FIGURE 4

Linear melodies may or may not possess formal symmetries, and
motivic melodies exist in which there are no variations or repetitions. These are called *through-composed melodies* and may result
through either contrivance or accident. Communication with the
listener is reduced by through-composed melodies and, though they
are sometimes effective, avoid them until you develop melodic

form and smoothly coordinated phrases through the study of the theme and variations technique.

Just as the young composer learns much about his craft by listening to music while following the score, the beginning improvisor can progress more rapidly by reading a transcription of an improvised solo while listening to the recording. If no transcriptions are available, you will have to transcribe them yourself, beginning with relatively uncomplicated solos and gradually trying more difficult ones. We cannot emphasize this practice too much; it will benefit you in two important areas: (1) it will develop your ear and pitch memory to the extent that you will eventually be able to transcribe *your own* ideas while you are improvising; and (2) by studying the solos and styles of already proficient improvisors, you will gain a deeper understanding of the improvised solo and will discover various methods and ideas for the handling of improvised material. Your sense for evaluating the merits of various soloists will also increase as you discover which solos can bear the careful scrutiny of analysis. Once the solo has been transcribed as accurately as possible, try to locate motifs, variations of motifs, and noteworthy linear sections, as shown in Figures 3 and 4.

In addition to studying solos through the use of transcriptions, it would be wise to begin an orderly and faithful collection of *original* motifs to be used for analysis and development. These will eventually become part of your jazz style and part of your repertoire of original ideas to be used in future improvisations. By studying Figure 3, you should get an understanding of the general appearance and nature of a motif. It is a short but complete melodic idea, usually having a logical rhythmic close, either by the use of a note of greater duration or by the use of rests. Anyone, even the beginner, is capable of composing short, original motifs, and with a little practice can become increasingly fast and accurate with putting them on paper. One or two motifs per day is reasonable as a beginning minimum. The output will increase naturally. The motifs should be neatly entered into a notebook (open to revision) and used as a source book of musical ideas. If you have difficulty composing motifs, you might begin by finding several pitches which sound good in succession and which seem to be relatively original, writing them as whole notes for the moment and adding a rhythm to them later.

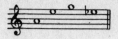 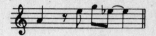

The ideas need not be striking or unusual. Don't wait for what you consider an exceptional motif to come to mind; even mildly effective ideas can become richer through thoughtful development, reworking, and variations. Simple, uncomplicated motifs are often more effective than more complicated ones. Furthermore, the ideas need not depict the style of "bluesy" jazz, with an abundance of lowered thirds, lowered fifths, and lowered sevenths, the ingredients often found in what is commonly termed a "funky" idea. The "funky" style will develop quite naturally in appropriate spots without encouragement, because of its popular usage and its suitability to the jazz style.

Successive, or at least well-placed, variations of motifs, when employed by the jazz improvisor, have a definite, strengthening effect upon the relationship between the performer and the listener. Richmond Browne, jazz pianist and instructor of theory at Yale University, wrote in a letter to the author:

What is the soloist doing when he attempts to "build"? Actually the ideal process hardly ever takes place—that is, it is hardly ever the case that a conscientious soloist plays a thinking solo for a hard-listening hearer—but when this does happen, the key process is memory. The soloist has to establish for the listener what the important POINT, the motif if you like, is, and then show as much as he can of what it is that he sees in that motif, extending the relationships of it to the basic while never giving the feeling he has forgotten it. In other words, I believe that it should be a basic principle to use repetition, rather than variety—but not too much. The listener is constantly making predictions; actual infinitesimal predictions as to whether the next event will be a repetition of something, or something different. The player is constantly either confirming or denying these predictions in the listener's mind. As nearly as we can tell (Kraehenbuehl at Yale and I), the listener must come out right about 50% of the time—if he is too successful in predicting, he will be bored; if he is too unsuccessful, he will give up and call the music "disorganized."

Thus if the player starts a repetitive pattern, the listener's attention drops away as soon as he has successfully predicted that it is going to continue. Then, if the thing keeps going, the attention curve comes back up, and the listener becomes interested in just how long the pattern *is* going to continue. Similarly, if the player never repeats anything, no matter how tremendous an imagination he has, the listener will decide that the game is not worth playing, that he is not going to be able to make *any* predictions right, and also stops listening. Too much difference is sameness: boring. Too much sameness is boring—but also different once in a while.

Most improvisors and composers have a natural inclination to use melodic form, but often to an insufficient degree. Both intellect and intuition must come into play if the solo is to be wholly satisfying. Methods for developing motifs should be studied, written, and played. If your original motif collection is used as a source for melodic development, it will follow that *all* the material developed from those motifs will also be original, and you will automatically develop an original style.

The only developmental method we will be concerned with in this chapter is *transposition,* which is simply a matter of rewriting a motif so that it fits another key, chord, or type of chord. Let us say that you have composed an effective motif which seems to fit nicely into the key of C. This means that the motif will serve you well, *as long as the piece begins and remains in C.* But of course not all tunes are likely to be played in the key of C, under normal circumstances; indeed, most tunes contain *at least* one simple modulation to another key. You certainly cannot afford to wait for a certain key, chord root, and chord type to use your motif. Furthermore, the continuity would be broken if you use it only at those widely spaced intervals. Therefore it would be well to learn to write and play your motifs in all keys (by transposition) and against all types of chords (by transposition and minor alterations, which will not affect the general character of the idea). Also, you will discover that many of your motifs can begin on another member of the accompanying or implied chord. To know what chord fits with a motif can seem like an overwhelming problem to the beginning student of improvisation. However, common sense and taste are the only guides to finding the "correct" chords; rarely can a motif be harmonized in one way only. This explains why a multitude of different chord progressions can (and do) exist on a single given tune when played by different improvisors of various styles.

To find an arbitrary chord which will fit the motifs, rearrange (if necessary) the tones used, being especially careful to include the important tones of longer duration (you will find that some can be omitted as embellishing, nonessential tones) so that they are stacked in third intervals as much as possible, simulating the construction of a triad or seventh chord. (Ninths, elevenths, thirteenths, and altered chords can be added when they become part of your harmonic knowledge.) Then analyze the resulting chord or chord fragment to determine the root and type of chord which should be used to accompany the motif.

Once the probable chord (or chords) has been determined, the motif is ready for transposition. Since the above motif is harmonized by an Em7, the first step would be to transpose it, raising it a half step each time (Fm7, F♯m7, Gm7, A♭ m7).

Now suppose, after having all the transpositions of the motif, you are confronted with an E7 rather than an Em7 chord. The motif, in order to fit a different type of chord, will probably require some alteration. There are many ways to vary the tones in the idea, without really changing its character. One way would be:

Regardless of the type of chord or the particular pitch of the root of the chord, the motif will adapt readily in a number of ways.

To add another dimension, it is usually possible to place the motif in a different area of the same chord or of a different chord. The motif under discussion begins on the root of the Em7 chord, but it could be revised to begin on the third (or fifth, seventh, etc.) of an Em7 chord (or any other chord or chord type, for that matter).

Once you have learned the motif in twelve keys, with M7, m7, and 7 chords, and built on at least two other members of the chord, you will have increased the number of useful circumstances for that motif (and some of these will offer interesting variations) from one situation to *one hundred and eight situations!* The transpositional possibilities for development are awesome and so may seem tedious to write; however you will find that you will soon be able to transpose quickly enough to dispense with writing them and simply play them in exercise form as preparation for their use in actual improvisation. An example of how these transpositions might appear in a solo would be:

Keep in mind that melodic variations have at least two objectives, both of which will raise the level of communication between the performer and the listener: that of offering contrast to the original version of the melody, and that of maintaining contact with the motif. By offering contrast, the variation extends the improvisation without risking boredom, and by having similarities to the original motif, the variation affords structural unity to the improvisation.

projects

1. Begin transcribing of solos, as suggested in this chapter.
2. Begin collecting of original motifs.
3. Learn to develop melodies by transposition, using the motif collection as a source of material.

3

the Rhythm Section

The rhythm section, because it provides the pulse, meter, rhythmic accents, compassionate or sympathetic balance, rhythmic "swing," and harmony, constitutes the heart of an improvising group. Some small jazz groups contain *only* rhythm section players —combinations of piano, bass, drums, and sometimes guitar, vibraphone, accordion, or Latin American instruments, such as conga drums, timbales, bongos, maracas, claves, guiro, cowbell, etc. In these cases the rhythm section must also supply *all* of the improvised solos and the foreground duties usually assigned to the wind instruments. In an optimum situation, when the members of the rhythm section are reasonably accomplished, their function is not simply to provide a throbbing background to a featured wind instrument, nor to play together in rhythmic and harmonic unison, as an indissoluble group. Rather they share the burden of the wind instrument by serving as a soundboard for its rhythmic accents, harmonic deviations, melodic continuity, and mood changes. They contribute more than their basic duties of time-keeping and background vamping by feeding the soloist with new material to be developed coordinately. At times they can even become cooperative entities within the rhythm section, echoing each other, dropping out occasionally, or becoming part of the foreground without necessarily involving the other members of the section. We shall limit our study to the basic foundations of rhythm section playing, as applied to the most common instrumentation of that section, the piano, bass, and drums.

drums

Contrary to common belief, the modern drummer does not rely upon the rhythmic figures of the bass drum or snare drum for maintaining the pulse (beat). He does, however, need to use some component of his drums for beating steady, dependable time, to which he can coordinate the improvised rhythms of the other components of his set. Oddly enough, the modern drummer, perhaps for the sake of subtlety, uses his cymbals for this purpose, either the "ride" cymbal (a large, medium thin, mounted cymbal), the "hi-hat" ("sock" cymbals), or both, played with either sticks or brushes. Although the patterns played on these cymbals can vary with the individual, the most common rhythm is:

If brushes are used, the ride cymbal pattern is often played on the snare drum with one hand, while the other hand rotates a brush around the edge of the snare head, making a "swishing" sound accenting the second and fourth beat by accelerating the swish sharply toward the body. The brushes can also be used on the cymbal, however.

The bass drum, snare drum, and tom-toms (if they are used), are usually reserved for improvised accents and this is left to the drummer's taste and discretion. Many drummers like to beat their bass drum lightly, even inaudibly, in steady quarter notes except when it is being used for accents. The pulse will be supplied by the string bass player, who will generally resent a heavily sounded bass drum which obscures the sound of the bass. In the unfortunate absence of a bass, a heavier bass drum is sometimes helpful, but it is unsatisfactory because of the short duration of its sound. Each of the pizzicato bass tones should have a long, singing sound.

bass

The rhythmic pattern of the bass is quite simple, usually quarter notes with occasional eighth-note figures to break the monotony. Once in a while the bass will play *in two* (quarter notes on the first and third beats) for a section of the tune, occasionally using quarter notes on second and fourth beats for variety.

As for the pitches played by the bass, there are several types of bass lines. The bass player's first obligation is to outline the consonant and important notes of each of the chords (especially roots and fifths), or he should at least outline the important notes of the tonality. The two most prominent types of bass lines can best be described as *chordal* and *scale-like* ("walking" line). The chordal line is the easier of the two and is recommended for beginners. The notes are chosen from the given chord, with emphasis given to the roots and the fifths. An example of such a line would be:

Note that the line contains practically no sevenths, but is more inclined to outline the triad portion of the chords. Because of the low range of the bass, the dissonance needs to be reduced by comparison with higher-pitched instruments. Simplicity and economy is of utmost importance for bass players, especially at the beginning. The line above would sound nearly as good even with successive repetitions of some notes. For example, the first measure could have been F, F, C, F, or F, F, C, C, instead of F, A, C, A (see example).

This is left to the taste, ingenuity, and technical ability of the player. The second and fourth beats can contain non-chord (dissonant) tones if the player so desires. For instance, the third measure could have been C, Bb, A, F, rather than C, F, A, C. It could even be C, Bb, A, G, since the non-chord tones would still be on the second and fourth beats. Traditional theory teaches us that both the metric and melodic accents in a quadruple meter (i.e. 4/4) occur on the first and third beats. This leaves the second and fourth beats unaccented, and therefore a logical place to use the nonharmonic tones of a melody. In *jazz*, the method for handling nonharmonic tones is essentially the same as in classical theory, but the metric accents are placed on the second and fourth beats. Consequently, the bass player should accent the second and fourth beats even though they might be dissonant (nonharmonic) tones. The first and third beats, of course, will be unaccented and consonant. It is best, when inserting non-chord tones, to choose tones within the scale of the key, hence the Bb instead of B.

The walking bass line is scale-like, using considerably more non-chord tones and even chromatic tones (tones not within the key signature). The walking line would look something like the following:

piano

The piano player is the one member of the rhythm section who has no definite rhythm pattern to maintain, yet his improvised rhythmic figures add greatly to the time-keeping. Perhaps the beginner should play in steady whole notes, half notes, or quarter notes, trying gradually to invent mixtures of these and to enhance them with syncopated figures. He should listen closely to the drummer for rhythmic figures which he can adapt. The soloing wind instrument may occasionally feed him possibilities also. The piano player should not be afraid to repeat figures once in a while, in a vamping style, changing the chords when necessary, while retaining the rhythmic figure. The pianist carries on three functions simultaneously: (1) the rhythm, including keeping tempo, maintaining the meter, and inventing interesting rhythmic "punches"; (2) the harmony; and (3) the element of melodic imitation, derived from the soloing instrument. He will soon learn, as the drummer does, that certain rhythmic figures will fit the meter, others will not, and experimentation will be his chief means of finding out.

He can, however, be prepared to play a variety of harmonic voicings by practicing them diligently, so that when the group assembles to play, his mind will be freer to concentrate on rhythmic figures and time-keeping. There are no set rules as to how he must arrange (voice) the tones of each of the chords; however there are certain tendencies established by taste and tradition which may be of help: (1) be flexible with voicings and strive for a variety; (2) try to avoid skipping by wide leaps when moving from chord to chord; (3) attempt, occasionally, to maintain the same top note, whenever it is common to several different chords, for at least several successive chords (all three of these points will encourage smoothness); (4) generally voice the root in the bass of each chord and space the chord wider near the bottom and closer near the top; and (5) use voicings of varying weight, depending upon the volume needed, playing fewer notes in softer passages and fuller-voiced chords in heavier passages.

Below are some suggested voicings for beginning pianists. Remember that these are suggestions for spacing and doubling that will apply to *any* type of chord, not just those shown here. These voicings should be practiced in all keys, on all types of chords. New ones should be invented and added whenever possible.

Voicing Code:	FM7	FM6	FM7	FM7	FM7	FM7
	7th	R	3	3	5	5
	5th	6	7	7	3	3
	3rd	5	5	5	7	7
	Root	3	3	3	5	R
	7th	6	5	7	R	
	Root	R	R	R		

projects

Drums. Practice alone, following the suggestions for the cymbal and hi-hat figures. Play *only* the cymbal and hi-hat at first, until this feels natural and until the tempo remains steady. Be sure to accent the second and fourth beats. Then try using brushes in either of the prescribed manners. When these time-keeping practices become easy and natural, and approach a subconscious level, try improvising accents with the snare and bass drum (letting them imitate each other and occasionally having them in unison) *but do not alter the cymbal and hi-hat figures while practicing improvised accents* and be sure the tempo remains steady. Practice various tempos like these.

EXAMPLES OF SOME POSSIBLE RHYTHMIC
FIGURES FOR SNARE AND BASS DRUM

Bass. Using the blues chord progression of Chapter 1, write several twelve-measure bass lines of both the chordal and walking type and practice playing them, striving for long pizzicato tones and a steady tempo. Transpose the lines to other keys and practice those. Practice various tempos.

Piano. Using the blues progression of Chapter 1, write and practice several twelve-measure voicings, keeping the type of voicing as consistent as possible. Play them in whole notes and half notes only, until a sense of meter develops, then try inventing various rhythmic figures which will fit the meter and which can be repeated for twelve measures.

4

the First Playing Session

Before assembling for the first playing session, each participant should prepare himself thoroughly by studying the material to be improvised. It should be memorized, even though a reference sheet will be placed before him. Each player should also practice the material diligently by inventing arpeggio and scale patterns for all of the chord symbols, covering the entire range of the instrument. If every person will study the material carefully *before* each playing session, then his mind and fingers will not be entirely taken up with the details of knowing what notes are in each chord, what scale is used with each chord, and how the phrases should be fingered. The mind and fingers will be free to concentrate on more important aspects of playing, such as establishing melodic form; developing the meter sense, mood, and swing; finding useful notes and phrases; and planning and controlling the intensity of a solo in chosen or inspired moments. None of these elements can materialize if the mind is struggling with chord and scale fundamentals. As the player develops, he will find that many of these aspects will become relatively subconscious and easy. Now he will be able to add even more objectives.

The reference sheet should look like Figure 2 (Chapter 1), except that it may need to be transposed to fit the keys of the variously pitched instruments. (For the first playing session, we will use the key of concert B♭, which will place B♭-pitched instruments in the key of C, and E♭-pitched instruments in the key of G.) The chord progression will be the same as in Figure 2, except for transposition. The reference sheet should be placed before each player in succeeding sessions until he feels confident that it is no longer necessary.

The members of the rhythm section should be seated as closely together as possible, and the wind instruments should be seated in a semi-circle, near the piano. The rhythm section should then play through the progression a few times, while the others watch their reference sheets closely, adjusting to the feeling of the tempo, learning to feel the durations of each of the chords, listening to the differences between successive chords, and trying to maintain the sound of the keynote in their minds. The pianist should play as simply and rhythmically as possible, sometimes playing whole note durations on the chords.

Next, the others should join in, playing several choruses of whole notes in unison, and playing only the roots of each chord.

This will train the player to hear the foundation of the progression and will help develop his sense of meter as he plays the harmonic rhythm (the relative duration of each chord). In this first session the harmonic rhythm is quite simple, since none of the chords has a duration shorter than a whole note.

The wind instruments should then be assigned a certain note of each chord to play for one chorus. For example, one could play the thirds of all the chords (in tempo), so that he would play (in concert key here) the following pitches in whole notes: D (third of B♭M7), G (third of E♭7), D, D, G, G, D, D, E♭, A, D, D. Another player will play all the fifths, another the sevenths, and another the roots. It won't matter too much which octave they choose for playing their assigned pitches, although it will sound best if the roots and fifths are in a lower range than the thirds and sevenths. After one or two choruses of this, exchange notes until each player has had the opportunity to play all the members of the chords. This exercise will strengthen the ear in understanding the sound of each of the chords, and will also teach you to think more quickly in terms of chord spellings.

Next, the wind instruments should play the following arpeggiated figure for several choruses (in unison):

This exercise begins to train the fingers to find correct pitches, though the pattern is repetitious. As explained in Chapter 1, habit plays an important role in improvising. By practicing exercises of this type, plus more of your own invention, you will form a foundation of correct finger habits. It is best that this type of exercise, as well as those described earlier, be practiced without reading, so that the intellect is encouraged toward deeper concentration.* Another exercise would be:

Eventually, when the progressions begin to move a little faster and half-note durations occur on some chords, such a pattern will have

---

* The development of concentration is a necessity for the improvisor. Not only will the player progress rapidly through complete concentration, but he will also learn to combat self-consciousness in performance. The accomplished improvisor has usually developed his powers of concentration to a very high degree. Mood and continuity are more consistently sustained when the player is not easily distracted. Also, a more technical and interesting performance is possible. By giving his attention wholeheartedly to the best possible contribution, the improvisor can relax quickly and dispense with the unnecessary physical effort that the rattled player must make. Advanced or gifted players may rely solely on emotion for total involvement. This is concentration of a type which transcends early technical training, and which eventually displays the musical personality of the artist.

to be revised, but once you begin to grasp the essence of these exercises, the invention of similar ones to fit new situations will not present a great problem.

The procedure just described should begin each playing session, especially when new material is attempted. The following summary can be used for future reference:

(1) preparation of the reference sheets before the session.
(2) study of the material by each student *before* playing.
(3) reading of the reference sheet while listening to the rhythm section play a few choruses.
(4) playing of roots in whole notes (or duration of the chords).
(5) playing of other members of the chords for their durations.
(6) playing of the chords in various arpeggiated figures.

Since you will feel some self-consciousness and confusion at the first session as to how to begin creating spontaneously, it would be helpful to work on an exercise which will dictate a simple rhythm and which will involve simultaneous improvisation by several students. The first improvisor could play a chorus of whole notes, followed by a chorus of half notes, then a chorus of quarter notes, and finally a chorus of any rhythm he chooses, but with eighth notes as the predominant rhythm. (This will also develop an orientation to rhythmic levels, so that you will be aware of whether whole notes, half notes, quarters, etc. are being played.) Choose any pitches, perhaps from the reference sheet at the beginning. Remember to use scale notes as well as chord notes, especially at the quarter-note and eighth-note levels. After the first player has completed his chorus of whole notes, the second begins playing his chorus of whole notes (while the first is playing half notes), then a third person begins playing whole notes, and so on. As each person completes his chorus of eighth notes he drops out until his turn comes around again to start another series of choruses like his first. When a fourth person begins playing, there will be four different rhythmic levels going on simultaneously, which will help relieve self-consciousness. This experiment, charted, would look like:

	Chorus 1	Chorus 2	3	4	5	6	7
1st Player	o —	♩ —	♩ —	♪ —			
2nd Player		o —	♩ —	♩ —	♪ —		
3rd Player			o —	♩ —	♩ —	♪ —	
4th Player				o —	♩ —	♩ —	♪ —
5th Player					o —	♩ —	♩ — etc.
6th Player						o —	♩ — etc.
etc.							

When you all feel comfortable in your playing situation, the preceding exercise can be eliminated in favor of several choruses each, accompanied only by the rhythm section. However, the above chart may be useful later in plotting ways to experiment with simultaneous and contrapuntal improvisation. It would also be advisable to transpose the progression used in this session so you will be able to play in all twelve keys.

This constitutes the rudimentary setting up of the first playing session. When the basic requirements for group playing become rote, then it is possible to bring in added considerations. For example, you should try to become aware of certain pitches within chords which seem more important than others in establishing chords and chord sequences. In examining the progression on page 5, we find that there is a need to clarify the third of the Bb chord as being major (D) rather than minor (Db). Similarly, the seventh of the Eb7 chord must be Db rather than D. The notes D and Db play a very important role in establishing the sound of the blues in the key of Bb. The blues progression has the peculiarity of seeming to shift between major *and* minor, without using a Bb minor chord. This effect is caused by the Eb7 chords, which contain the Db's that would have been the most important note of a Bb minor chord, had there been one. Then the primary function of the Eb7 chord is to create a feeling of Bb minor in the second, fifth, and sixth measures of the blues progression.

Another important pitch in the B♭ blues is the E♭ that occurs as the third of the Cm7 chord in the ninth measure, and as the seventh of the F7 chord in the tenth measure. This E♭ strengthens the key feeling of B♭, yet it also delays the resolution to the tonic (B♭M7) chord, which is one of the few notes which cannot be sounded consonantly with a B♭ chord. In conclusion, the three important notes in the blues lie within the small area of a major second from D♭ to E♭, and the charting of these important notes would be:

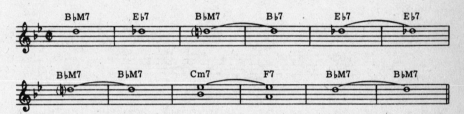

You may now begin to notice that if you play the notes of the chord in rapid succession as pickup notes to a phrase, it becomes easier to hear what should be played. Tonal memory is much like eyesight in that an impression is made which lingers. A tone registers long enough to retain the sound of a chord for a while after the sound has stopped. When a chord is played in arpeggiated form, the sound is established long enough to be heard simultaneously with subsequent notes. Eventually you will find that you need play only the more important notes of a chord to establish the sound of the entire chord. These notes will usually be the third and the seventh, because their chromatic position determines whether the chord is a M7, m7, or 7, while the fifth and root usually remain stationary.

Notice that in the diagram given above for the Cm7 and the F7 there are two pitches given as important; the B♭ to A have not yet been discussed. When either a m7 or a 7 chord resolves to a seventh chord which is located a perfect fourth above (from C to F is a perfect fourth), the most effective way to establish the joining of these chords is to move from the seventh of the first chord (B♭ in the example, since it is the seventh of the Cm7) to the third of the second chord (A, which is the third of an F7). The reason for this is that the other notes of the Cm7 chord—C, E♭, and G—could be the

fifth, seventh, and ninth of the F chord and are inconsequential because they are stationary during the change of chords.

If any of the players has difficulty improvising with a particular
chord, let the pianist strike the chord and hold it (not in tempo)
until the player can improvise a number of useful phrases.

As the beginning improvisor finds certain phrases he likes to use
from time to time, he is confronted with the problem of fitting the
phrase into the meter, so that it starts and ends at the proper time
within the measure. For example, suppose you like to play a
B♭M7 in this way:

Now suppose you arrive (in a continuous line) at the junction of
your previous idea and this phrase, but a little too early or too late.
Always be prepared to cope with these unexpected situations by
improvising a few pitches which will enable you to place the idea
where it metrically should be. Therefore, instead of turning out
like:

it might be:

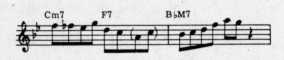

or:

or:

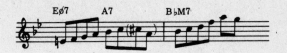

It is also suggested that in future sessions you prepare some of the motifs from your collection, transposing them and altering them slightly so that they can be used in improvisations at *any point*.

project

Write an original solo on the blues progression, in any key, one chorus in length, using one or two (only) motifs from your collection of motifs. Strive for naturalness of style.

5

Development of the Ear

When a student of music theory identifies and writes what his instructor plays for him in a dictation exercise, he is using the same process used by the jazz improvisor. He is translating abstract sound into tangible symbols and making it understandable. The student is translating sounds coming to him through the auditory senses and placing these sounds (in symbol form) on paper. The improvisor is working with imagined sounds which, when translated, are played on his instrument. The mechanical process of translation, however, is the same and can be developed through extensive practice. Figures 5 and 6 are illustrations of these two types of dictation.

With composers, the process is nearly identical to that of the improvisor, except that the brain translates the imagined sounds into symbols to be placed on paper. The important thing to note is that in *any* case, the main process is the same, that of dictation. If the student of jazz can transcribe what he hears from an outside source, he can translate what he hears from an inner source through the same developed technique of taking dictation. Therefore, if he practices transcribing music, regardless of the style, he will greatly increase his ability to improvise. The improvisor will often need to use his transcribing ability to translate the sounds around

34

him in an improvising session if he is to fulfill his obligations toward group improvisation, and if he is to learn from listening and *understanding* the efforts of those around him.

sound

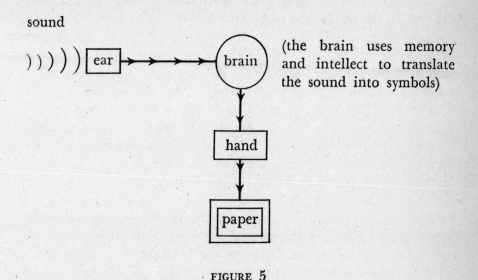

(the brain uses memory and intellect to translate the sound into symbols)

FIGURE 5

Dictation from an Outer Source

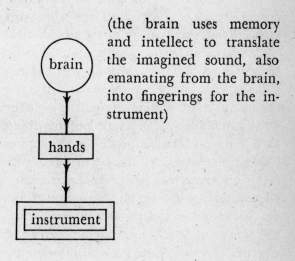

(the brain uses memory and intellect to translate the imagined sound, also emanating from the brain, into fingerings for the instrument)

FIGURE 6

Dictation from an Inner Source

The memory plays an important part in that it must record imagined sounds instantly so that they can be taken in dictation before the images disappear. Successful efforts can be retained in the memory from one session to another. Improvisation, like composition, is the product of everything heard in past experience, plus the originality of the moment. The contents of even a very accomplished improvisor's solos are not all fresh and original, but are a collection of clichés, established patterns, and products of the memory, rearranged in new sequences, along with *a few* new ideas.

A valuable aid to the improvisor is the development of relative pitch on his instrument. This enables the brain to make efficient, accurate translations of heard pitches (from either an inner or outer source) into fingerings necessary to produce that pitch on the instrument. A player who has used his instrument to transcribe melodies (especially if the melody is played on the same type of instrument) has probably discovered that each pitch on his instrument has a slightly different tone color from the others. For example, most pianists can tell when the black keys on a piano are struck in a sequence containing mostly white keys. They can also hear a great difference between pieces played in the key of D♭ and pieces played in the key of E, usually describing D♭ as dark, heavy, and morose, and E as bright, brilliant, and light. String players can often detect a change of strings when listening to another player, especially if the type (gut, metal, wound, and so forth) of string changes within a line. Saxophone, clarinet, and flute players can recognize a difference in quality at the register changes (where the player moves between pitches requiring few or no fingers, to pitches requiring many fingers, though the pitches may be only a minor second interval apart). These minute differences in quality can lead to a type of relative pitch which applies only to the particular instrument played by the performer. It can be developed through dictation exercises (using the instrument, rather than committing the material to paper) and the memorization of the qualities found on various pitches of the instrument. After the improvisor develops this sense of pitch to a high degree, he will find that he can identify the exact pitches on different instruments by hearing the note played as it would sound on *his* instrument and identifying it by quality. This is why many saxophone players who switch from an Eb-pitched instrument to a Bb-pitched one are unable to improvise with ease, especially if they use only their ear to guide them. They find themselves playing pitches that are a perfect fourth away from the pitches they intended to produce. Since the fingerings are the same on the new instrument, he has not made allowance for the fact that the two instruments are pitched a perfect fourth apart.

The advantages of acquiring keen pitch perception on a particular instrument are many. First, it practically eliminates all errors involving pitch translation. Second, it enables the player to become proficient in the area of melodic imitation in group situations. Third, the player becomes adept at comprehending the unfamiliar harmonies of new tunes, or different progressions to already learned material. Last, and perhaps most important, the improvisor is aware, on the first hearing, of the exact pitches used by other performers.

To develop this most invaluable aid to improvising, it is suggested that you adopt the following methods:

(1) Begin observing the slight differences in the tone quality of various pitches and registers on your instrument.
(2) Meet with another player of the same instrument and practice tone-matching exercises, beginning with one pitch at a time and gradually working toward longer series.
(3) Begin transcribing from recordings of solos of your instrument, playing them on the instrument rather than committing them to paper.

Remember that developing this sense of pitch is a long-term project and that progress may be slow.

6

Further Study of Chord Types

Up to this point, we have used only three types of chord structures, the M7, the m7, and the 7 chords. Frequently, for the sake of variety or to harmonize melody notes which are not within one of the preceding chord structures, alternate chords are used. As will be pointed up in Chapter 10, there are three main functional categories of chords, and the three we have taken up so far are the most commonly used chords of each of the families.

In place of a M7, for example, a *M6 chord* may be substituted. The M6 chord is like the M7 in that it uses a major triad for the bottom three notes, but adds the sixth major scale degree instead of the seventh. A CM6, then, would be spelled C, E, G, A.

If the tune used in an improvisation is in a minor key, then it is necessary to learn a type of minor chord, especially to be used as a tonic minor chord, which differs in sound and construction from the m7 chord. There are two basic examples of this tonic minor sound, the *m6 chord* and a *minor chord with a major seventh* (interval), which we will call a *m♯7* or a *m♮7* (depending on whether it is necessary to use a sharp sign or a natural sign to show how the seventh has been raised). A Cm6 chord would be spelled C, E♭, G, A, and the Cm♮7 would be spelled C, E♭, G, B♮ (not B♭, as in the Cm7).

Sometimes a m7 chord may be replaced by a *half-diminished seventh chord* ($\phi7$) which differs from the minor seventh chord only in that the fifth is lowered a half step. A $C\phi7$ chord, instead of being spelled C, E♭, G, B♭ (Cm7), is spelled C, E♭, G♭, B♭.

A $Cb5$ or a $C+5$ may often be used in place of a C7; they are spelled C, E, G♭, B♭, and C, E, G♯, B♭ respectively, rather than C, E, G, B♭.

All the newly given alternate chords may be used in place of their given and more common chord family member (M7, m7, or 7) quite freely, sometimes depending upon the harmonization of a given melody. A summary of the families is given below.

M7	'Tonic Minor'	m7	7
M7	m6	m7	7
M6	m♯7 or m♮7	ø7	7 +5
			7 ♭5

Figure 7 shows a summary of the symbol, name, intervallic construction, and an example of each of the chord types included thus far.

Most of the newly added chords, though they belong to families of already learned chords, will require scales different from those given in Chapter 1 for the M7, m7, and 7 chords. It will be remembered that a major scale was used for the M7 chord, a Dorian Mode for m7 chords, and the Mixolydian Mode for the 7 chord, the constructions of which are given in Chapter 1.

The M6 chord will use the same scale as the M7 chord. However, the m6 and m♯7 (or m♮7), depicting the minor mode, will differ from either the M7 or m7 in respect to the scale used with it. The ascending form of the melodic minor scale (see p. 40) may be used with either the m6 or the m♯7 chords, as the scale contains all the notes of those chords. The harmonic minor scale (see p. 40) may accompany the m♯7 chord only, since the lowered sixth degree would conflict with the sixth of the m6 chord.

SYMBOL	NAME	INTERVALS CONTAINED	EXAMPLE
M7	major seventh chord	major third perfect fifth major seventh	CM7 
M6	major sixth chord	major third perfect fifth major sixth	CM6 
m6	minor sixth chord	minor third perfect fifth major sixth	Cm6 
m♮7 or m#7	minor chord with a major seventh	minor third perfect fifth major seventh	Cm♮7 
m7	minor seventh chord	minor third perfect fifth minor seventh	Cm7 
ø7	half-diminished seventh chord	minor third diminished fifth minor seventh	Cø7 
7	seventh chord or dominant seventh chord	major third perfect fifth minor seventh	C7 
7+5 or +7	augmented seventh chord	major third augmented fifth minor seventh	C+7 
7♭5	seventh chord with a diminished fifth	major third diminished fifth minor seventh	C7♭5 

FIGURE 7

40

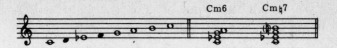

C melodic minor scale (ascending)

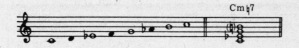

C harmonic minor scale

The scale which best fits the ø7 chord is one which uses the notes of a major scale of a half step up (called Locrian mode), hence a scale on B would use the notes of a C major scale, but starting on B (B, C, D, E, F, G, A, B). This type of scale contains all the notes of a ø7 chord built on the root of the scale.

Locrian Mode on C (D♭ major scale, starting on C)

One appropriate scale fits both the +5 and ♭5 chords—the *whole-tone scale,* which, as its title suggests, is constructed by using successive whole steps *only.*

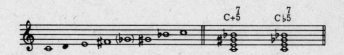

C whole-tone scale

A summary of all the types of chords, their families, and their accompanying scales is given below for quick reference.

Chord Family	Chord	Scale
M7 (Tonic Major)	M7 ...... Major Scale M6 ...... Major Scale	
Tonic Minor	m6 ...... Ascending Melodic Minor Scale m♯7 ..... Ascending Melodic or Harmonic Minor Scales	
m7	m7 ...... Dorian Mode* ø7 .... Locrian Mode	
7 (Dominant)	7 .... Mixolydian Mode 7 +5 .... Whole Tone Scale 7 ♭5 .... Whole Tone Scale	

Jazz is a relatively new art whose language and symbols are still in the process of becoming standardized. Consequently, the student of improvisation could easily become confused by encountering unfamiliar symbols found in chord progressions given him by players of another geographical location. Some of the deviations one might expect to encounter are:

$$M7..........Maj.7, \quad \triangle 7$$
$$m7...........-7$$
$$ø7...........m♭5, \quad \begin{matrix}7 & -7\\ & -5\end{matrix}$$
$$M6..........6$$
$$7.............x7$$

Figure 8 shows a new progression to the blues, this one in the minor mode and using some of the chords introduced in this chapter. This should be transposed for the various instruments

* Traditional modal terminology is given because it is unnecessary to coin new terms for an old scale system.

and used as a reference sheet for the next playing session. The scheduling of playing sessions from this point is left to your own discretion. There is no limit to the number of possible sessions, but one should be scheduled at least whenever there is new material to be assimilated.

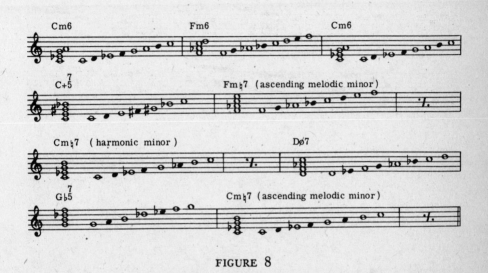

FIGURE 8

projects

1. Write and practice (in arpeggiated form on the instrument) the
   $$M6, m6, m\#\overset{7}{7}, (or\ m\natural\overset{7}{7}), \emptyset 7, +5, \flat 5\ chords\ in\ all\ keys.$$

2. Write the melodic minor, harmonic minor, Locrian Mode, and whole-tone scales in all keys. (There are only two whole-tone scales. You will find the others are all repetitions of one or the other.)

3. Above each of the written scales, write the chord root and chord type which can be used in conjunction with the scale.

4. Transpose to all keys and practice the following pattern of scales. Play continuously, stopping only for breath.

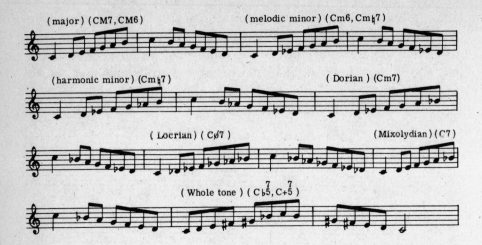

7

Swing

One quick way to determine the depth of a jazz musician's thinking is to ask him to define *swing*. Even some of the most articulate jazz critics and chroniclers will avoid a penetrating discussion of swing and generally back themselves into a corner when they do engage in one. Yet many who are concerned with jazz, when asked to name the most important aspect of jazz music, will exclaim "Swing!" and will even minimize the importance of other aspects, such as melodic form, functional harmony, technical proficiency, a well-developed ear, versatility, originality, and so on. There is no question as to the controversy in an analytical discussion of swing, perhaps from uncertainty more than anything else. Furthermore, if you want to watch artists nearly come to blows, try standing a few feet away from the members of a rhythm section during an intermission, if the group is having problems with swing. The issue becomes even more complicated when the necessary *intensity* of swing is discussed.*

Swing is a combination of two things: rhythmic interpretation and rhythmic unity. Steady tempo should also be considered, but it is known that some jazz groups will swing while the tempo changes

---

* The intensity of swing can vary greatly in the styles of different jazz musicians—indeed, it can even vary at times within a single individual. The tunes and arrangements can also call for more or less intensity of swing. Intensity of swing can be determined by any one, or a combination, of these factors: (1) dynamic level or loudness; (2) mood or time-feeling; (3) unity in the sense that all members of a performing group are playing with the same concept of the pulse. With these variables, it is easy to see how individual tastes might conflict on such an issue.

unintentionally. Some jazz artists have even contended that the tempo is *never* steady, that the swing is partly due to a flexible, rather than a metronomic beat. (African rhythms, which are supposedly the origin of jazz rhythms, are characterized by gradual accelerandos in near perfect unison.) Other jazz players, even those who feel that swing is the most important ingredient of jazz music, believe that swing, though of a different type, exists in a good symphonic orchestra or chamber group, because there is an emotional or interpretational type of unity. The intensity of the swing feeling in any kind of music should be flexible enough to range from blatant to subtle, depending upon the mood and demands of the particular selection or player.

Unfortunately, young jazz players are often told that they must *first* learn to swing, even in the beginning stages of improvisation. This is analogous to expecting the beginning archer to score consistent bulls'-eyes before attempting the outer circles. The relaxation and coordination necessary in playing swing usually cause swing to become the *last* added element rather than the first. The person who swings at the outset is indeed rare and fortunate, as it indicates rhythmic and emotional precocity and will probably insure easier progress and acceptance.

Rhythmic unity must come naturally through compatible combinations of rhythmically competent individuals experienced in playing together. However, the rhythmic interpretation of the jazz improvisor's most consistently used rhythm, the eighth-note pattern,

can be learned to a reasonably accurate degree through purely technical means, those of rhythm, articulation, and accents. Rhyth-

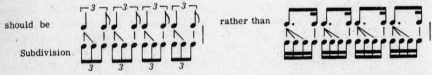

mically, the dotted eighth-sixteenth–note pattern has often been supposed to be the rhythmic interpretation of the eighth note as played by improvising or reading jazz artists. However, the effect is too jerky to be used in place of the preceding examples, because the beat is subdivided into four parts, rather than three.

The music is seldom written either of the above ways but usually in straight eighth notes with the interpretation left to the improvisor, who usually plays them as he would in improvising. This rhythm is sometimes referred to as *shuffle-time*.

Although most jazz music is legato or legato tongued, there is a tendency among improvisors to attack lightly every other note, slurring to the ones between, using the tongue *on the upbeats* and slurring into the downbeats. This articulation probably had as its source the peculiar upbeat accent which is a distinguishing trait of the jazz style (therefore the preponderance of syncopated figures) and which would be somewhat facilitated by a tongued rather than a breath accent.

There are, of course, deviations from rhythmic interpretation, articulation, and accents, but these three aspects are prevalent. Now let us work with a line which might be played by an improvising jazz artist, first playing the line as it is written, without altering the rhythm, articulation, or accents.

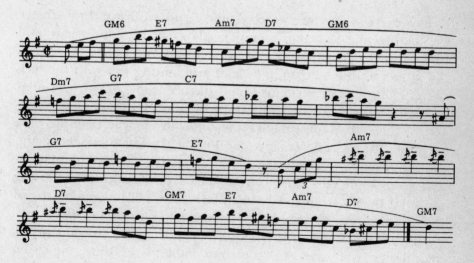

FIGURE 9

Although the chosen pitches seem to be well within the jazz style, swing is almost totally lacking when the line is played without a jazz interpretation. Now play the line again, this time using the shuffle rhythm, but still not inserting the jazz articulation or accents. It will be noticed this time that a feeling of swing is beginning to affect the line, when it is played like:

Next add the articulation as in the example below, maintain the shuffle time, but leave out the accents.

Finally, add the upbeat accents to complete the study.

This exercise may seem too technical and mechanical to achieve the total feeling of swing; some jazz players, critics, historians, and listeners feel that swing cannot be analyzed and taught. However, the success of this exercise in at least acquainting you with the feeling of swing cannot be denied, and further study along these lines will have an even greater impact on the ability to swing. It is suggested, then, that you practice the following longer example of a jazz line. If necessary, practice the line in the same manner as the previous example, adding the rhythmic interpretation, articulation, and accents one at a time, unless you have no difficulty practicing all three aspects at once. However, be careful not to exclude any of them. From time to time you may come upon phrases which cannot be played exactly as prescribed here, but as long as the rhythm, articulation, and accents are present most of the time, the swing feeling will persist.

FIGURE 10

projects

1. Practice playing Figures 9 and 10, following the prescribed procedure for interpretation.
2. Assemble the group for a session and perform Figures 9 and 10, using the given progressions. Practice them in unison at first, then have each person perform the line, followed by an improvised chorus, attempting to carry on the feeling of the written choruses into the improvised chorus. (Both Figures 9 and 10 are blues progressions in G and C major respectively; Figure 9 is one chorus in length, and Figure 10 is two choruses.) Because of the difference in key signatures, the two figures should of course be taken up as separate selections.

the Diminished Scale

The use of various scales in jazz is a fascinating subject. George Russell, jazz pianist and author of *The Lydian Chromatic Concept of Jazz Improvisation,* focuses his method on scales, rather than chords, as a means of organizing tonal materials. In a system of this sort, the improvisor uses scale references (including many alternate scales of graded dissonance) in improvisation and uses chords only as a means of determining the scale possibilities. The improvisor depends more upon his ear to guide him through the chord notes that will best make the harmonic progression clear. The over-all emphasis is on the development of a strong linear style.

The *diminished scale* is a peculiar scale alternating, in construction, between whole steps and half steps.

C Diminished Scale

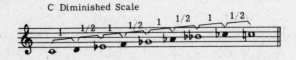

It was omitted from Chapter 6 because of its more complicated structure, and because its unusual ability to fit several types of chords would have caused some confusion to the reader. However the increased usage and popularity of the diminished scale prohibits its exclusion from a text on jazz improvisation, and so we will devote a short chapter to its origin, construction, and usage.

The diminished scale derives its name from the *diminished seventh chord*.

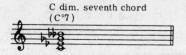

This chord is constructed of successive minor-third (1½-step) intervals, giving it a kind a symmetry in appearance and an ambiguity of sound that has perplexed many theorists and composers as to its use in harmony. Because of its unique structure (having no intervals usually found in harmony based on tonic-dominant relationships), it sounds key-less and the listener has some difficulty anticipating the next chord. In fact, the diminished seventh chord can resolve to almost any chord and sound reasonably acceptable. It can even resolve to another diminished seventh chord. Indeed, since any of the four notes could be the root, the root cannot be determined by sound, but only by analyzing the spelling of the chord. It most often functions as a substitute for a 7 chord built on the seventh degree, by omitting the root and adding a minor third interval above the seventh.

The ambiguity of the diminished seventh chord carries over in the diminished scale, creating a very flexible, colorful, effective, and practical scale. (Note that the second, fourth, sixth, and eighth scale degrees of the diminished scale form another diminished seventh chord, located one step above the prementioned chord.) It is important to remember that the scale always has a whole step as its first interval. If a half step is used first, another diminished scale will be formed, but it will not apply to the same situations as the diminished scale beginning with a whole step, because the root of the scale will have changed. There are only three different diminished scales, if we dispense with enharmonic spellings (E♯/F,

Bb/A#, C#/Db, etc.), i.e. C, Db, and D, because the Eb diminished scale will contain the same tones as the scale on C, the scale on E will duplicate the pitches found in the Db diminished scale, and so on.

The diminished scale naturally sounds best with a diminished seventh chord. It also sounds good enough with the ⌀7, m6, m#7, and m7 chords, to be used as a colorful second choice of scale for those chords, using the same root for both scale and chord (that is, D diminished scale for D⌀7, F diminished scale for Fm7, G diminished scale for Gm6 or Gm#7, and so on).

However, the most effective use of the diminished scale with chords commonly used in jazz, is in its application to the 7 chord. The 7 chord in jazz, as we will discover in Chapter 10, often contains altered tones which do not change the function of the chord, but which enrich the over-all quality of the sound. You are already familiar with 7 chords which have a raised or lowered fifth. Later you will find that ninths, elevenths, and thirteenths, and their alterations, are frequently added to the 7 chord. It would be safe to say, then, that, of the commonly used jazz chords, the 7 chord has the greatest potential for harmonic richness. If an Ab (½ step up from G) diminished scale were applied to a G7 chord (or a G $\flat$5), the total harmonic effect would be created by a root, third, fifth, seventh, lowered ninth, augmented (raised) ninth, augmented eleventh, and thirteenth! Thus, only two chord notes of the possible ten—the augmented fifth and major ninth—are not produced by the diminished scale. (The diminished fifth is the same as the augmented eleventh, except that the latter is an octave higher.) If the chord is a G+5, then a whole-tone scale would be used, and if the chord includes a major ninth, either a whole-tone scale or a Mixolydian Mode could be used, depending upon the presence of a lowered or raised fifth. It is very important to remember that the G7 uses an *Ab diminished scale*, rather than a diminished scale built on G.

It is also interesting to note that when the diminished scale is applied to the 7 chord, there are no tones which act *only* as joiners *between* chord tones. *All* the tones are chord tones or altered chord tones.

Figure 11 outlines all the seventh chords, the chord families, and the choices for accompanying scale.

Family	Chord	Scales		
		First Choice	Second Choice	Third Choice
Tonic Majors	M7	major scale		
	M6	major scale		
Tonic Minors	m6	melodic minor	diminished	
	m♯7	melodic minor	harmonic minor	diminished
m7	m7	Dorian Mode	diminished	
	ø7	Locrian Mode	diminished	
7 (Dominant)	7	Mixolydian Mode	whole tone	diminished (1/2 step up)
	7 +5	whole tone		
	7 ♭5	diminished (1/2 step up)	whole tone	
	ø7 (M3 up)	diminished (on chord root)		

FIGURE 11

projects

1. Write and practice the three different diminished scales. Add this scale to the scale exercise given at the end of Chapter 6.
2. Find the diminished scale used in Figure 10 of Chapter 7.
3. Write and practice, in arpeggios, the three different 7 chords.
4. Review, in a playing session, the various blues progressions (major and minor) given up to this point, inserting the diminished scale whenever possible. Be sure that the scale root is identical to the chord root, except in the case of 7 chords and 7 chords with a lowered fifth, where the scale root will be one-half step above the chord root.

9

Analysis and Development of Melody

By now you should have collected a number of original motifs and should be familiar with transposing and altering motifs to fit any given material or key. In this chapter you will learn to take motifs apart and to rebuild related material from the constituents.

In order for you to understand a motif fully and to realize its potential for development, we will describe it by shape (contour), the relative sizes of its pieces (rhythm), and its outstanding features (essential pitches).

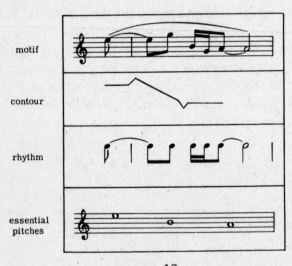

FIGURE 12

We can get an even clearer picture of the motif by analyzing it for prominent intervals, implied harmony, articulation, phrasing, and mood. However, at this point these considerations are secondary to the more important and useful aspects of contour, rhythm, and essential pitches.

Just as the ingredients of the motif may be removed and examined apart from the whole, so can these elements be regarded as outlines for reconstructing (singly or in ensemble) a slightly different motif, but one which still bears resemblance to the original idea. In this way the two motifs (or a whole section) are held together by means of an almost invisible thread of memory and logic. We discover, upon analyzing a number of ideas, that the different components seem more important with some motifs than with others. If the player wishes to follow one idea with another which bears strong resemblance to it, then he will use the more essential element. If he wishes the second motif to be a more subtle echo of the first, then he may employ one of the lesser characteristics.

Figure 13 shows two examples of melodic development by contour. The contour is a line which describes the spacial motion of the motif. If it describes it adequately, then another motif may be invented which uses the same contour. It is not limited to the same pitches or rhythm, yet this new idea will give strong reminiscences

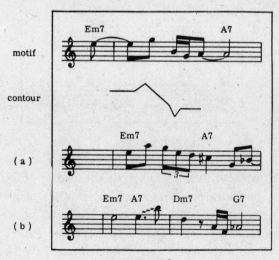

FIGURE 13

of the one from which its contour was derived. Let the ears decide what the new pitches should be, and the eyes and intellect will check the contour and prevent errors in pitch choices. Always play the original motif and the development in succession, in order to determine whether or not the development is a successful imitation.

Contours can also be used in another way. They can be invented, rather than taken from an existing motif, simply by your drawing or imagining an interesting contour and then composing an idea to fit it. Then, by repeating the contour, inventing a new sequence of pitches with each repetition, you establish a feeling of melodic form.

The rhythm of a motif can be handled in much the same manner, as shown in Figure 14, by composing a new idea from the rhythmic pattern of the original motif. It is not necessary to use the contour of the first motif, nor is it imperative to use the essential pitches of the first melody.

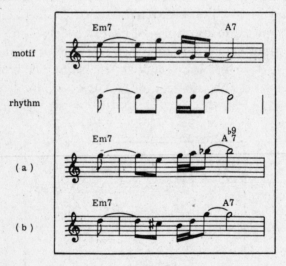

FIGURE 14

Developing a formful melody through the use of essential pitches is a little more challenging. The essential pitches of a melody are the most important notes of that melody, the ones which might be retained in the memory after only one hearing. The least important and less memorable notes are weeded out by the ear and the intellect. Since these pitches are likely to be missing in the next change of harmony, melodic development by essential pitches is best used in tunes which have repetitious chords, so that the pitches will apply to the harmony for a greater duration and can be repeated severally. In rare cases it might be possible to transpose the essential pitches to fit a new set of chords, but the intervals created by the essential pitches must be striking enough to be reminiscent in the new setting. In creating a new set of secondary pitches with which to surround the essential ones, the essential pitches can accidentally be subjugated or weakened by any new pitches which are: (1) higher in range; (2) accented; (3) placed in strong rhythmic positions; (4) given greater durations; (5) repeated; or (6) approached by leaps (wide intervals). These possibilities should be used to strengthen the *essential pitches,* and should be avoided when subordinate notes are added. Figure 15 gives two examples of melodic development through the use of essential pitches. The method for determining the success of this type of development is a check to see, after playing the new idea, that the successive motifs appear to have the same essential pitches as the original one.

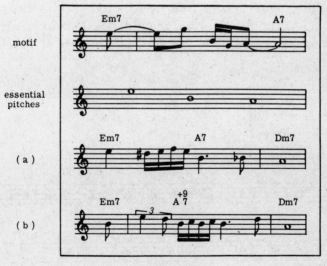

FIGURE 15

The object, in the case of development by transposition, contour, rhythm, or essential pitches, is the same: to establish melodic form by repeating some aspect of the original motif, and then composing new sequences of intervals to supply the needed variety. As in the case of the contours, a rhythm may be invented, without relating it to an already conceived idea, and used as an outline for the creation of a melody.

projects

1. Analyze each of your collected motifs in the manner shown in Figure 12.
2. Write at least three examples of each of the development methods (transposition, contour, rhythm, and essential pitches), using the analyzed material from Number 1 above. Use any harmonic foundation you choose.
3. Try improvising (alone) more examples of melodic development along the lines of the examples you have just written.
4. Using the progression given below, write a full chorus of successive developments of a *single motif,* trying each of the development techniques at random within the tune. Strive for naturalness and uncontrived continuity. Study the example given below the progression for guidance, but do not feel compelled to imitate its style, contents, or sequence of development methods.

Concert key
Transpose if necessary
to key of instrument.

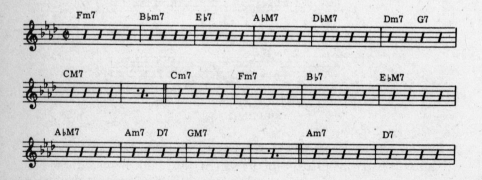

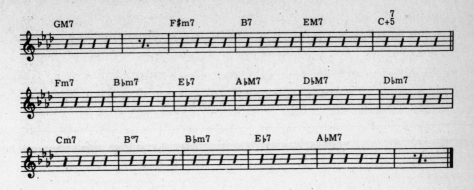

Example

5. Practice and discuss the chorus developed above at the next playing session.

6. During the session, and after everyone is familiar with the progression used for Project 4, cite any motif from your written chorus and have *everyone* improvise developments of that motif in their own choruses. Repeat the process with other players' written choruses.

7. Transpose and make up a reference sheet for the progression given below. Practice improvising the tune in a session until

everyone is comfortable with it. Then try improvising to the given contours (individually, with the rhythm section), changing to the next contour every eight measures, so that each person will work with all four contours within each chorus. Remember that the duration of the individual contour is left to the improvisor, so that there is no reason why each contour or repeat of a contour needs to be a certain number of beats in length. Furthermore, rests can be inserted at the discretion of the player.

Concert key

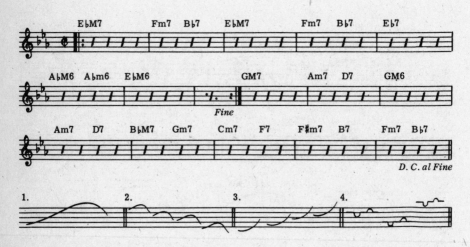

8. Using any blues progression in any key, let each improvisor play three choruses, using (a), (b), and (c) of Series I (below) as the rhythmic framework for his improvisation, playing each figure for a full chorus. The contours and pitches are left entirely to his desires, but each rhythm should be carefully adhered to for the full twelve measures. After all have played, repeat the process for Series II. The drummer should either be playing the figures lightly behind each person or be ready to play it, should the player lose his place. When everyone has learned to handle the rhythms in Series I and II, then the miscellaneous rhythms in Series III should be tried, alloting a full chorus for each rhythm.

series i

(a)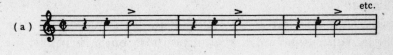

(b)

(c)

series ii

(a)

(b)

(c)

series iii

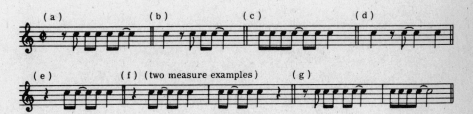

9. In Figure 10 (Chapter 7), find two measures which are identical, except for the transposition necessary to make the idea fit the chord.

10. In Figure 9 (Chapter 7), locate a similar example of two measures which differ *only* in transposition, but which have identical contours, rhythm, and intervals.

10

Chord Superimposition

Ninth, eleventh, and thirteenth chords are produced by super-imposing third intervals above the seventh chord, thereby adding color and a thicker texture to the seventh chord without changing its function. This practice is commonly used in jazz, because the extension of the seventh chord provides more harmonic choices.

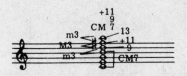

Note that the ninth degree above the tonic corresponds to the second degree, except that it is written an octave higher; in like manner the eleventh and thirteenth correspond to a fourth (aug-mented fourth, in this instance) and sixth scale degree, respectively. These superimpositions have a certain potential for alterations, as do the third, fifth, and seventh of the seventh chords. It is up to you to remember which types of chords can use ninths, elevenths, and thirteenths, and which of these superimpositions can be altered in certain chords. The superimposition is considered unaltered if it is within the scale that accompanies the chord.

Figure 16 shows many possibilities for superimposition on the various types of seventh chords used in jazz. Group B includes both

POSSIBLE SUPERIMPOSITIONS

BASIC CHORD	Ninth (9)	Diminished Ninth (♭9)	Augmented Ninth (+9)	Eleventh (11)*	Augmented Eleventh (+11)*	Thirteenth (13)*
Group A M6 M7	CM6 9 CM7 9	ill - advised	ill - advised	ill - advised	+11 9 CM6 +11 CM7	M6 - superfluous (M6 = 13) 13 +11 9 CM7
Group B m6 m7 m♮7 or m♯7 ø7	Cm6 9 Cm7 9 Cmø7 9 Cø7 9	ill - advised	superfluous (m3 = +9)	11 9 Cm6 11 Cm7 11 Cmø7 11 Cø7	ø7 - superfluous (♭5 = +11) m7, m♮7, and m6 ill - advised	m6 - superfluous (M6 = 13) ø7 and m7 ill - advised 13 +11 9 Cmø7
Group C 7 +7 7 ♭5	9 7 C7 9 C+7 7 C♭5	♭9 7 C7 ♭9 C+7 7 C♭5	+9 7 C7 +9 C+7 +9 7 C♭5	ill - advised	7 ♭5 - superfluous (♭5 = +11) +11 9 7 C7 +11 C+7	+7 ill - advised 13 +11 9 7 C7 13 +11 9 C+7 7 C♭5

64

the tonic minor chords (m6 and m♯7) and the minor sevenths (m7 and ø7) because both categories have about the same potential for ninths, elevenths, and thirteenths. Group A contains the tonic major chords and Group C contains the 7 (dominant) chords. It is common practice among jazz musicians to add more than one superimposition to some chords, when possible, or eliminate any one or two superimpositions in favor of the remaining one(s). It is easy to see that the possibilities for variation are many.

The 7 chord has one more superimposition possibility than the other members of Group C (+5 and ♭5) and is more flexible than all the chords in Figure 16, in that it can endure more superimpositions, altered and unaltered, than any of the other chords, without the loss of its function. Only thirteen combinations are listed for Group C, but in reality there are twenty-one possibilities, if we were to include the altered forms of the ninth in the eleventh and thirteenth chords. The additional eight would be:

In using the more complicated chords shown in Figure 16 and the additional eight shown above, you will become aware of new problems, aside from that of memorizing the possible superimpositions on various types of chords in all keys. (It is taken for granted that this material would be overwhelming if tried, with all its possibilities, within a single session. It will have to be digested gradually over a long period of time.) As you will discover, these superimpositions often do not sound well when played abruptly and

---

FIGURE 16 (opposite)

* The ninths were left in, even after the elevenths and thirteenths were added, and the elevenths usually remain after the thirteenths had been added. This is not necessary.

** The ninths of the eleventh and thirteenth chords in Group C could have been diminished ninths or augmented ninths.

by themselves. Find ways to approach these notes from simpler chord notes in such a way that the added ninths, elevenths, or thirteenths are related to something in its proximity which is consonant. Otherwise, the superimposition may sound awkward, detached from the harmony, or simply incorrect. At the beginning it is suggested that you precede these added notes with several successive and more consonant chord notes, perhaps as pickup notes to a phrase.

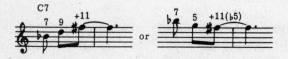

You will also discover certain melodic formulas for handling these pitches, once having arrived at them. For example, the augmented eleventh sounds well when it is followed by an embellishing figure containing the thirteenth and the octave of the fifth.

Another example would be to precede an augmented ninth with the third and follow the augmented ninth with a lowered ninth.

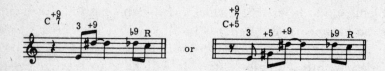

Some of the superimpositions sound best when approached from above, others are best when approached from below, and sometimes it depends upon the pitches used in conjunction with the note. These will evolve out of your experiments in improvisation, and there is no way of guaranteeing that what sounds pleasing to you will also please everyone else, or even yourself at a later date.

If we extract the ninth, augmented eleventh, and thirteenth from a C chord, we have the notes D, F♯, and A, which spell a D major triad. Therefore, if we want to add a major ninth, augmented eleventh, and thirteenth to *any* chord, we simply add a major triad whose root is a major second (one whole step) above the octave of the chord's root. Now we are no longer thinking in terms of superimpositions of ninths, elevenths, and thirteenths, but are involved instead with *polychordalism,* which is the simultaneous playing of two (or more) different chords. In this case we have a D major triad over a C seventh chord. There are several advantages to thinking polychordally, especially if you know what triads over a seventh chord will create the effect of superimposed ninths, elevenths, and thirteenths. This approach is faster, easier to handle, purer in sound, and it increases the number of altered pitches possible on any chord. (For example, B, D♯, F♯—the members of a B major triad—sound well, and have been used by many jazz orchestrators, over a CM7 chord, creating an augmented ninth with the D♯, a sound which was ill advised in Figure 16. This exception is perhaps due to the fact that in polychordalism the two chords are heard separately, and also due to their usual separation in range from each other.) The chart shown in Figure 17 gives a multitude of acceptable major and minor triads over the four families of seventh chords. In parenthesis after each superimposed triad possibility is the effect, in terms of ninths, elevenths, and thirteenths, created by that superimposed triad.

To illustrate the use of the chart in Figure 17, let us say we are given a 7 chord to play in a particular section of a tune, and suppose we would like to use a triad which will give the sound of a seventh chord with an augmented ninth. We look for the horizontal column containing triads for seventh (dominant) chords. In the first box to the right we find this alteration given in parenthesis after m3. Since this box is in the vertical column of major superimposed triads, the desired triad will be a major triad whose root is a minor third above the root of the seventh chord. Suppose that the given seventh chord is a B♭7 chord. A minor third above B♭ is D♭, so our superimposed triad will be a D♭ major triad (D♭, F, and A♭), which will give us the sound of a B♭7 with an augmented ninth. (D♭ is the same as C♯, the augmented ninth of B♭.) If the given chord is a GM7 and we wish to know what triads we can superimpose over that chord, we first locate the proper family (tonic

FOUNDATIONAL (GIVEN) SEVENTH CHORD - TYPE	LOCATION (BY INTERVAL ABOVE ROOT OF FOUNDATIONAL SEVENTH CHORD) OF ROOTS OF SUPERIMPOSED TRIADS	
	MAJOR TRIADS	MINOR TRIADS
* TONIC MAJOR	M2 ↑ [13, +11, 9, M 7] P5 ↑ [9, M 7] M7 ↑ [+11, +9, M 7]	M7 ↑ [+11, 9, M 7]
TONIC MINOR	M2 ↑ [+11, 9, m 6] or [13, +11, 9, m #7] P5 ↑ [9, #7, m 6] or [9, m #7] M7 ↑ [+11, #7, m 6] or [+11, m #7]	M2 ↑ [11, 9, m 6] or [13, 11, 9, m #7] M7 ↑ [+11, 9, #7, m 6] or [+11, 9, m #7]
MINOR SEVENTH	m7 ↑ [11, 9, m 7] or [11, 9, ø7]	
** DOMINANT SEVENTH	M2 ↑ [13, +11, 9, 7] m3 ↑ [+9, 7] d5 ↑ [+11, b9, 7] m6 ↑ [+9, 7, +5] M6 ↑ [13, b9, 7]	m2 ↑ [b9, 7, +5] m3 ↑ [+11, +9, 7] d5 ↑ [13, +11, b9, 7]

M = major interval (up)
m = minor interval (up)
P = perfect interval (up)
d = diminished interval (up)

(2, 3, 6, and 7 intervals are called *major,* if unaltered from major scale, *minor* if lowered one-half step. Four and 5 intervals are called *perfect* if unaltered from major scale, *diminished* if lowered.)

FIGURE 17

* Only the major seventh chord is given here, though the same triads can be superimposed over the M6 chord as well.
** Only the 7 chord is given here, though the same triads can be superimposed over the 7 chords with a +5 or b5 as well.

major), which is in the upper left-hand corner of the figure. By moving horizontally to the right we find that we can use major triads built a major second up from our GM7 (A major triad), a perfect fifth up (D major), a major seventh up (F♯ major), or a minor triad built a major seventh up from G (F♯ minor triad). Choice of these depends upon personal likes and needs.

To notate, in a progression, the existence of a superimposed triad, the foundational seventh chord symbol is written, a short horizontal line is placed above it, and the superimposed triad symbol is placed above the horizontal line.

Example: $\dfrac{C\sharp}{B7}$ or $\dfrac{C\sharp M}{B7}$ $\dfrac{Bm}{CM7}$ or $\dfrac{B}{CM7}$

Below are some possible ways to use polychordalism in improvised phrases.

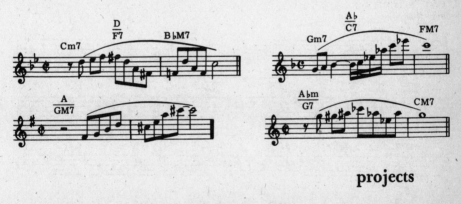

projects

1. *Group exercise in chord building.* The first person chooses any pitch of the chromatic scale for a chord root. The second player places a third (major or minor, as he chooses) on the chord. The next places a fifth on the chord, being careful that the type of fifth fits with what has gone before. The fourth person gives the chord a seventh that is possible with the triad that has been built up to now. (Now the chord can be mentally categorized by everyone into one of the four seventh chord categories.) Next a ninth is added, *if it is possible* (a °7 chord, for example, cannot take a ninth), and so on, until everyone has had a turn, then the

first person carries on from there and starts another cycle. Each person *must* have the chord in mind, so that he does not add a note which is not possible. When nothing more can be added to the chord (which will not always happen on the thirteenth), then the chord is finished. The one who correctly identifies the chord chooses the root to be used in the next chord.

2. Transpose the following progression (if necessary) for a playing session. Write superimposed triads of your choice *above each measure* for the first twelve measures of the progression and another set of triads above each measure for the first eight measures of the repeat. Make a separate copy in concert key for the piano player. Try using these triads in the session. NOTE: the bass player should always remain on the foundational seventh chord, and the pianist should play the foundational seventh chord with his left hand and the superimposed triads with his right.

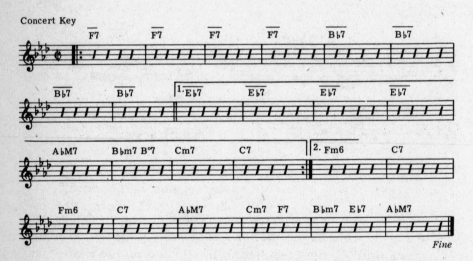

3. Find two places in Figure 10 (Chapter 7) in which a minor triad of a minor second (up) has been superimposed over a 7 chord.
4. Find examples of augmented ninths, lowered ninths, and augmented elevenths in Figure 10 (Chapter 7).

11

Functional Harmony

It would be possible, having learned the chord symbols and chord structures found in jazz, to dispense with any further consideration of jazz harmony. However, this would be analogous to learning the alphabet and vocabulary of a foreign language and, without knowledge of the syntax or structure, attempting to speak the language. It would be helpful to learn the functions of the four families of chords (actually there are only three, since the tonic majors and the tonic minors function in the same way, establishing the tonic in the major and minor modes), as well as to gain an understanding of the functional sequence of chords.

The tonic chords are like magnets, tugging at the other types of chords, giving the dominants and minor sevenths tension that must be resolved. The tonic is the only chord which offers complete rest. The dominants are so near to the tonic that they are intense and powerful, and must be resolved to the tonic. The minor sevenths, which function as *subdominants,* are remote from the tonic and act as a secondary tonic, offering repose, but not inertness. Therefore, subdominants lead to dominants, which move to tonics or back to subdominants. Once the progression reaches the tonic it usually ends or starts another cycle by moving out to a subdominant.

71

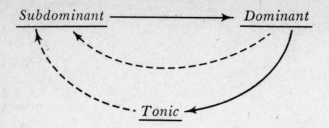

The application of roman numerals to the lettered chords of all keys makes for easy comparisons of chord progressions. We will call the tonic chord I, and the chords built on the second, third, fourth, fifth, sixth, and seventh scale degrees are numbered II, III, IV, V, VI, and VII, respectively. If the chord root is located between scale degrees, then a flat or sharp sign may be placed before the roman numeral. For example, a chord whose root is between the second and third scale degree could be called either a #II or a ♭III chord. Then to complete the symbol, we simply add our signs to indicate M7, M6, m6, m#7, m7, etc. Suppose that one progression is in F# major, another is in A major, and a third progression is in E♭ major, and their progressions are as follows:

(F#)	G#m7	-	Bm6	-	A#m7	-	D#7	-	G#m7	-	G7	-	F#M7
(A)	Bm7	-	Dm6	-	C#m7	-	F#7	-	Bm7	-	B♭7	-	AM7
(E♭)	Fm7	-	A♭m6	-	Gm7	-	C7	-	Fm7	-	E7	-	E♭M7

We might guess that the progressions are similar because the *types* of chords agree; however, the root progressions are difficult to compare because of the distantly related keys. Now translating the root progressions into a common language, the roman numeral system, designating the keynote as I in each example, we find that they are identical progressions.

IIm7 - IVm6 - IIIm7 - VI7 - IIm7 - ♭II7 - IM7

The problem of transposing chord progressions for playing sessions is greatly reduced if the progression is given in roman numerals, even if the tune contains modulations. The player need know only the interval between the two keynotes and he is prepared to write a parallel modulation for a different-pitched instrument. For example:

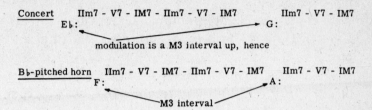

The letters below the progression, of course, are of greatest importance, since they designate the key, the location of modulations, and the relative position of the new keynote. If the tune is in a minor key, lower case letters are used (b instead of B, f♯ rather than F♯, and so on).

Modulations to another key are sometimes very difficult to recognize. Yet it is important to do so in order to achieve a clear understanding of chord progression tendencies. For example, suppose you analyzed the above progression, translating lettered chord roots into roman numerals, but were unaware that the tune modulated up a major third interval at one point. Your analysis would be:

Lettered Roots	Fm7 -	Bb7 -	EbM7 -	Fm7 -	Bb7 -	EbM7 -	Am7 -	D7 -	GM7
Translated to	IIm7 -	V7 -	IM7 -	IIm7 -	V7 -	IM7 -	♯IVm7 -	VII7 -	IIIM7
Eb:									

You would still find the correct chords when you played, but you would be led to believe that $\sharp IV^{m7}$—VII^7—III^{M7} are common chords and that the Am7, D7, and GM7 chords are functioning, somehow, in the key of Eb. Both of these assumptions would be incorrect. Those particular roman numerals are very uncommon, especially in groups. One might occur by itself, functioning as a passing chord between two more common chords, or as a substitution for a common chord, but it is highly unlikely that more than two such chords would appear. The Am7, D7, and GM7 chords function not in the key of Eb, but in the key of G major.

In searching for possible modulations while translating lettered symbols into roman numerals, the following questions might be asked:

(1) Are there any spots where it has been necessary to place flats or sharps before the roman numeral? If so, a modulation might be present.

(2) Are there a considerable number of roman numerals which are *not* I, II, or V? This could indicate the area of a modulation.

(3) Are there some I chords which are not I^M, II chords that are not II^m, and V chords that are not V^7? If so, this could also be pointing up a modulation.

(4) If the answer to questions 1, 2, or 3 is "yes," is there a M7 or M6 chord on a tone which is *not* I or IV? If there is, this could be the tonic of a new key. You might also check to see if there is a tonic minor chord in the questionable area.

(5) If a tonic chord has been found on a scale degree other than I or IV, are there, preceding that, chords which could function as II^{m7} or more especially V^7? If so, a modulation is certain; try to locate the exact point where the previous key became hazy and the new key began to emerge. Under the first chord definitely belonging to the new key, whether or not it is I, place the letter of that key, followed by a colon (i.e., G:) and relate the roman numerals from that point to the new position of I.

The keynote or tonic chord needs relief, as its inertness and monotony can weaken a progression. Consequently, many tunes contain a simple modulation up a perfect fourth, making IV sound like a new tonic in a new key. However, in most cases the modulation is temporary and the progression falls back to the original tonic within a measure or so, the modulation having served its purpose. The relationship of keys separated by a perfect fourth (i.e. C and F) is so close that, unless a modulation to that nearly related key is sustained, it would perhaps be inaccurate to consider it as a modulation in the true sense of the word. Therefore, we will take the liberty of maintaining the original keynote as I throughout modulations up a perfect fourth, and a common progression such as the following:

CM7	-	Dm7	-	G7	-	CM7	-	Gm7	-	C7	-	FM7	-	Fm6	-	CM7

will become:

IM7	-	IIm7	-	V7	-	IM7	-	Vm7	-	I7	-	IVM7	-	IVm6	-	IM7

C :

rather than:

IM7	-	IIm7	-	V7	-	IM7	-	IIm7	-	V7	-	IM7	-	IVm6	-	IM7

C :   F :   C :

(The chord which leads back to I is often a $\sharp IV^{o7}$ or a IV^{m7} followed by a $\flat VII^7$, rather than the IV^{m6} that is shown here.)

In translating lettered symbols into roman numerals, either for the purpose of understanding the functions of the chords or for simplifying transposition, you will need to know which roman numerals and their chord-types are most common. By now you are probably aware that I^{M7}, II^{m7}, and V^7 chords are going to be prevalent, since they are considered to be the most important chords in establishing a new key, as shown in the discussion on recognizing modulations. Since temporary modulations to IV are common, expect also to find some V^{m7}, I^7, and IV^{M7} chords, as well as the IV^{m7} used to return to I. Below are listed the most common chords found in jazz tunes, listed in the order of their frequency of occurrence. You will, of course, also encounter others.

Chord Function (most common function)

comprise approximately 75 per cent of all chords

1. V^7 ...... Dominant of I
2. II^{m7} .... Functions as subdominant of I, precedes dominant, and is substitute for IV
3. I^{M7} ..... Tonic
4. VI^7 .... Precedes II
5. III^{m7} ... Substitutes for I. Often follows V^7
6. VI^{m7} .... Substitutes for I. Often follows I or occurs between III and II
7. I^7 ...... Dominant of IV
8. IV^{M7} ... Tonic relief. Temporary (usually) key center
9. V^{m7} .... II^{m7} of IV. Usually precedes I^7 (dominant of IV)

10. IV^m7 .... Transitionary chord between IV^M7 and I^M7, or between II^m7 and I

11. II^7 ..... Sometimes substitutes for II^m7. Usually occurs between VI^7 (or VI^m7) and V^7

12. ♭III^m7 .. Substitutes for VI^7. Usually occurs between III^m7 and II^m7

13. ♭VII^7 ... Usually occurs between IV^m7 and I^M7

After you have translated the lettered chords of a tune into roman numerals, your next step is to study the tune for its *general functional structure,* by grouping portions of the progression into areas of the tonic, dominant, or subdominant, and grouping together measures that move the tune into another key. Figure 18 shows two examples of tunes by jazz composer-pianist Duke Ellington, which have been plotted in terms of areas of the tonic, dominant, and subdominant. This does not say that the chords will all be I, V, or IV chords, but that the functions of the other chords can be classified in the general area of the tonic, dominant, or subdominant.

mood indigo

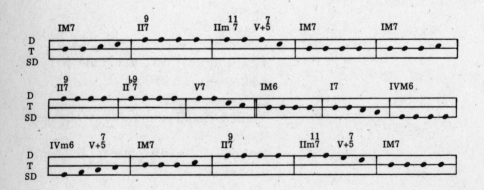

take the "a" train

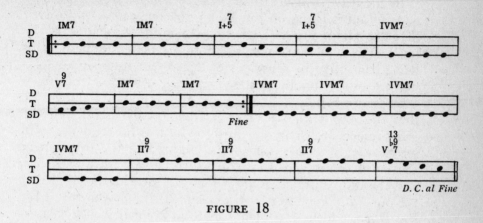

FIGURE 18

The grouping of measures into sections which have a key in common could be illustrated by projecting the tune used in Project 4 of Chapter 9.

In discussing functional harmony, Richmond Browne dismisses the importance of superimpositions of ninths, elevenths, and thirteenths, and states the problem as being that of knowing when the harmony is generally in the tonic, dominant, or subdominant, or in a nearly related key. Browne writes,

> The only thing left of a tune after it has really been worked over in modern jazz is the general *functional* structure—in very broad terms, too. The exact root progression is usually gone; the melody is gone, but the number of bars in the tune remains the same, and you generally reach the tonic, dominant, or subdominant in the same measures as they occur in the original version of the tune. All substitutions, fake cadences, or tricks cannot obscure the recognizability of that structure. Therefore, the student should grasp this fact firmly,

and have it in mind—that the functional structure of a tune is its identity. The details of exactly which form of a dominant sound is going on can be approached more fruitfully if they are all treated as variants of a position relative to the tonic. The endless variety of chords is better thought of as being controlled by questions of density, or sonority, or spacing, and not harmony in the sense of voice-leading. Example: I place my hands on the keyboard at random, making sure that the lowest note I strike is functionally useful, but the other fingers are spaced in thirds or fourths for sonority, or in seconds for bite. My harmony is limited to the function of the lowest note, and maybe a fifth or a seventh above that, and the rest of the notes are color. . . . Bearing in mind that the one *basic harmonic urge* seems to be the movement of the root *down* a fifth (a tendency more prominent in jazz than in classical harmony, from which it is derived), it is seen that the *basic harmonic problem* is to get above the tonic functionally and create suspense by delaying the resolution.

It will be found that jazz harmony makes great use of the cycle of fifths in progressions. (This could just as easily have been called a cycle of fourths. If you go downward in successive perfect fifth intervals, you will arrive at the same pitches as you would by going *up* in successive perfect fourth intervals.)

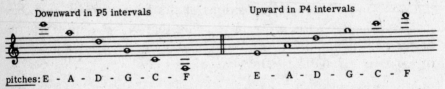

Downward in P5 intervals   Upward in P4 intervals

pitches: E - A - D - G - C - F   E - A - D - G - C - F

The chord sequences may vary the cycle by adding or eliminating a chord or two, and the progression may abruptly move to a remote place from the previous chord, but the pattern established by the cycle of fifths will generally show through all the variations. Figure 19 shows this cycle in two forms, in letters and in roman numerals. The chord-types in such a chain will vary.

Examine the tune in Project 4 of Chapter 9 and note that the first five measures follow the cycle of fifths (either in lettered symbol or roman numeral form) perfectly by using the root sequence

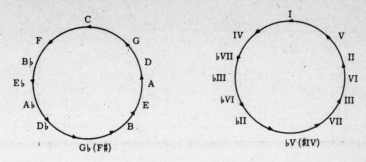

FIGURE 19

F, Bb, Eb, Ab, and Db. In the next measure we find another chain, starting on D, continuing to G, C, F, Bb, Eb, and Ab. The common progression of IIm7, V7, IM7 is a clear example of the cycle of fifths, and this progression is often extended to become IIIm7, VI7, IIm7, V7, IM7, which is an even longer cycle.

The next most common tendency in chord progressions is for the roots to move chromatically downward, as in the interpolation of a bIII chord between a IIIm7 and a IIm7 chord. Sometimes a long chain of chromatically moving chords will occur in a tune, such as C7, B7, Bb7, A7, and so on. A few progressions even contain sections where the root movement is chromatically upward, but the tendency for downward chromaticism is much stronger. The root sequence which is least common is the movement upward or downward by whole steps.

If you wish to alter a progression without disturbing its objectives, Figure 20 can help you make your choices for substitutions. Theoretically, you should be able to move from any of the chords in the subdominant class, to any of the chords in the dominant category, and finally to any of the chords in the box containing the tonic chords and tonic substitutions. The most common way of moving through these groups would, of course, be IIm7—V7—IM7. However, it would be possible to use a bII7, for example, in place of the V7. Another possibility would be IVM7—#IV°7—IIIm7, which would avoid all three of the more common chords. Note that the direction of progression in the figure is from right to left, rather than from left to right.

TONIC	DOMINANT	SUBDOMINANT
IM7 or IM6	V7	
	VII°7	IIm7
IIIm7	♭II7	
	#IV°7	
VIm7	#II°7	IVM7 or IVM6

◄————————————— Direction of Progression

FIGURE 20

projects

1. Translate the tune given in Project 4 of Chapter 9 into roman numerals. Do the same for Project 7 of that chapter.
2. Quiz yourself on the functions of the 13 common chords listed in this chapter, covering the right-hand column with a piece of paper.
3. Plot the first eight measures of the tune in Project 7 of Chapter 9 in the manner shown in Figure 18 of this chapter, then plot out the key sequence for the entire tune.
4. Memorize the cycle of fifths, then find sequences from that cycle in the tunes given in Projects 4 and 7 in Chapter 9.
5. Revise the chord progression of Figure 10 (Chapter 7), using the above substitution chart as a guide.
6. Read Appendix A and discuss with jazz enthusiasts. Listen to some prominent jazz players on record and discuss their work in terms of the criteria listed in Appendix A.
7. Pianists. Work on the left hand suggestions in Appendix B.
8. Study the material in Appendix C and experiment with it in playing sessions.
9. Study the tunes and tune-types presented in Appendix D. Make reference sheets on them and play them in sessions. Play them in the order in which they appear.

Appendix A

Aesthetic Criteria for the Evaluation of a Jazz Artist

Since the growth of the student of jazz will depend to a great extent on the influence of recorded music, he must learn to absorb and evaluate what he hears. His assessment of techniques will in time become automatic and he will then be free to perceive the music from every aspect. Jazz is made up of many intangible qualities that create appeal. This appeal becomes a matter of personal taste. However, there are some definite questions that the listener can ask that are necessary to a well-rounded evaluation.

1. *Choice of Materials.* Does the artist make use of the best songs available? Is the song appropriate for the player's style and interpretation?
2. *Emotional Content.* Does his tone quality seem alive? Is he able to project, emotionally?
3. *Versatility.* How many different moods is he able to create? Does he adapt to new musical environments and establish rapport with others in the group? Is the excitement he creates limited to swing, rhythmic outbursts, humor, and mischief? Or does the excitement also take on the more subtle aspects of beauty, thoughtfulness, sincerity, sweetness, and melancholy?
4. *Taste.* Is the chosen mood always appropriate to the musical situation? Does he practice moderation and economy in using his materials and techniques?

5. *Originality*. Is the artist an innovator? Though he might show that he has absorbed the qualities of other players, is there a considerable amount of material which seems to be his own, so that one is actually able to distinguish him from other artists of a similar style? Does there seem to be a creative urge about him which causes his style to be constantly enriched with new ideas?
6. *Intellectual Energy*. Can the player hold one's interest with only the stimulus of his ingenuity? Is the player physical, cerebral, or both?

Appendix B

Since jazz is a relatively new form of expression, there exist certain problems which still need to be solved through theory and practice. One of these problems is the harmonic coordination of the piano player's left hand with the bass player's lines. Most pianists use their left hand to accompany the melodies improvised by their right. The left hand plays chord roots (as bass notes), along with one or two other chord notes above the bass note, which are usually a seventh and possibly a tenth (wide reach of octave above the third). If the pianist's left-hand bass note coincides with the root played by the bass player, there is an intonation problem, plus the interference with the bassist's tones by the doubling of his tones in the same or near octave on the piano. If the left-hand piano bass note does not coincide with the string bass note, then it is reducing the clarity and freedom of the bass line. In conclusion, it would be helpful to the over-all sound of an improvising group if a new type of left hand were developed which would not use roots as bass notes and which would be separated from the string bass range.

Such a solution has been developed by several leading jazz pianists, whose left-hand styles contain no roots, except for final cadences, leaving the bassist full freedom of range and style. Examples of some of these left-hand chord voicings are shown in the remainder of Appendix B.

Some Possibilities for Voicings

Tonic Majors

3rd in bass   5th in bass   7th in bass

Tonic Minors

3rd in bass   5th in bass   7th in bass   9th in bass

Subdominants

3rd in bass   5th in bass

7th in bass   9th in bass   11th in bass

Dominants

3rd in bass   5th in bass

7th in bass   9th in bass

an Example of Usage in a Blues Progression

(Left Hand)

Alternate Chord Progression to the Blues

	1	2	3	4	5	6	7	8	9	10	11	12
(a)	IM7	IV7	IM7	I7	IV7	IV7	IM7	IM7	V7	V7	IM7	IM7
(b)	IM7	IV7	IM7	Vm7 I7	IV7	#IV°7	IM7	VI7	IIm7	V7	IM7	IM7
(c)	IM7	IV7	IM7	Vm7 I7	IVM7	IVm7	IIIm7	VI7	IIm7	V7	IM7	IM7
(d)	IM7	IIm7 #II°7	IIIm7	Vm7 I7	IVM7	IVm7 bVII7	IIIm7	bIIIm7 bVI7	IIm7	V7	IM7	IM7
(e)	IM7	VIIø7 III7	VIm7 II7	Vm7 I7	IVM7	IVm7 bVII7	bIIIM7	bIIIm7 bVI7	IIm7	V7	IM7	IM7
(f)	IM7	IV7	IM7	bIIIm7 bVII7	IVM7	bVm7 VII7	IIIm7	VI7	IIm7 V7	bVIm7 bII7	IM7	IM7
(g)	bII7 bV7	VII7 III7	IM7	V7 I7	IV7	#IV°7	IIIm7	bIIIM7	bVIM7	bIIM7	IM7	IM7
(h)	Im6	IIø7 V+5⁷	Im6	I7	IVm6	IVm6	Im6	Im6	IIø7	V+5⁷	Im6	Im6
(i)	Im6	IIø7 V+5⁷	Im	Vø7 I7	I7	#IV°7	Im6	bIIIm7 bVI7	IIø7	V+5⁷	Im6	Im6

85

Common and Similar Chord Progressions often Used as the "A" Section of a Tune Having an A-A-B-A Structure

	1	2	3	4	5	6	7	8
(a)	IM7	IIm7 V7	IM7	IIm7 V7	IM7 I7	IVM7 #IV°7 V7	IM7	IM7
(b)	I VIm7	IIm7 V7	IM7 VIm7	IIm7 V7	Vm7 I7	IVM7 IVm7	IM7	IM7
(c)	IM7	IIm7 #II°7	IIIm7 VI7	IIm7 V7	Vm7 I7	IVM7 #IV°7	IM7	IM7
(d)	IM7 VI7	bVI7 V7	IM7 VI7	bVI7 V7	Vm7 I7	IVM7 IVm7	IM7	IM7
(e)	IM7 bIII7	II7 bII7	IM7 bIII7	II7 bII7	Vm7 I7	IVM7 IVm7	IM7	IM7

Two Common Types of "B" Sections, with their Deviations often Found in Tunes Having an A-A-B-A Structure

type i

(a)	III7	III7	VI7	VI7	II7	II7	V7	V7
(b)	VIIm7	III7	IIIm7	VI7	VIm7	II7	IIm7	V7
(c)	III7	IVm7 bVII7	VI7	bVIIm7 bIII7	II7	bIIIm7 bVI7	V7	bVIm7 bII7
(d)	VIIm7 III7	IVm7 bVII7	IIIm7 VI7	bVIIm7 bIII7	VIm7 II7	bIIIm7 bVI7	IIm7 V7	bVIm7 bII7

type ii

	1	2	3	4	5	6	7	8
(e)	I7	I7	IVM7	IVM7	II7	II7	V7	V7
(f)	Vm7	I7	IVM7	IVM7	VIm7	II7	IIm7	V7

Common Turnarounds*

(a) IIIm7　VI7　　IIm7　V7

(b) IM7　VI7　　♭VI7　V7

(c) IM7　♭III7　　II7　♭II7

(d) IM7　♭IIIM7　　♭VIM7　♭IIM7

(e) IM7　♭II°7　　IIm7　V7

(f) IM7　♭VII7　　IM7

(g) IM7　　♭IIIM7

* A *turnaround* is a short series of chords, occurring at the close of a segment of a tune, which replaces an extended duration of a tonic chord. This relieves possible monotony and serves to prepare a repeat of a section or chorus.

a Collection of Tunes, Categorized According to their Characteristic Progressions

PART I

TUNES HAVING SIMILAR BEGINNINGS

A. Tunes which begin on a II⁷ chord

(Medium fast)

(1) II7 · V+5⁷ · IM7 · VI7 · II7 · V+5⁷ · F:

I7 · · IVM6 · #IV°7 · IM7 · VI7

II7 · | 1. IIm7 · V7 : | 2. V+5⁷ · IM6 ·

(Moderately)

(2) II7 · IIm7 · V7⁹ · IM6 · II7⁹ · F:

IIm7 · V7 · bVII7⁺¹¹ · VI7 · bIII° · IIIm7 · VI7 · IIm7 · V7

1. IM7 · VIIø7 · III7 · VIm6 · II7 · IIm7 · V7 :

2. I7⁽ᵇ⁹⁾ · IVM6 · #IV° · IIIm7 · VIm7 · IIm7 · V7⁹ · IM6 ·

(Slow)

(3) II7⁺¹¹ · I7⁺¹¹ · II7⁺¹¹ · I7⁺¹¹ · VI7 · IIm7⁹ · Ab:

V7⁺¹¹¹³ · IM6 · · IIm7⁹ · bII7⁺¹¹ · IM7 · VI7 · IIm7⁹ · V+5⁽ᵇ⁹⁾⁷ · Fine B:

IM7⁹ · IVM7 · IIm7 V7 · IM · VIm7 · Im7 · IV7⁺¹¹ · D: D. C. al Fine

(Medium fast)

(8) Ab:
II7⁹ V7¹³ IM7⁹ IM6 I7⁹

IVM7⁹ IVM6 IVM6 bVII7⁹ IM7

II7 1. IIm7 V7 2. IIm7 V7 IM6

(Slow)

(9) Eb:
II7⁹ IIm7⁹ V7¹³ IM7 VIm7 IIIm7¹¹ VI7 II7⁹

IIm7⁹ V7¹³ IM7 Vm7¹¹ I7 IVM6 IVm6 V7♭⁹

IM7⁹ VI+5⁷ II7⁹ IVm♮7 IIm7¹¹ V7⁹ IM6

B. Tunes which have I^{M7} to IV^7 as their first two chords

(Fast)

(10) Bb
IM6 IV7 II7

IIm7 V+5⁷ IM6 Vm7 I7⁹

IVM6 II7 V7
D. C. al Fine

(Very fast)

(11) Bb:
IM6 IV7¹³⁹ IIIm7 VI+5⁷

IIm7⁹ V7¹³ IM6⁹ Vm7 I7 IVM7⁹

bVIIm7 bIII7 VIm7 II7⁺⁹ bVIm7 bII7
D. C. al Fine

(Fast)

(12) $\|:$ IM7 / / / / | IV7 / / / / | IIIm7 / / / / | VI$^{\flat 9}_{7}$ / / / / | II7 / / / / |

B♭:

V7 / / / / | IIIm7 VI7 / / | IIm$^{11}_{7}$ V+$^{7}_{5}$ / / $:\|$ | IM7 / / / / | IIm7 V+$^{7}_{5}$ IM7 / $\|$

D:

I 7^{13} / / / / | VII 7^{13}_{9} / / / / | ♭VII7 / / / / | VI7 / / / / | ♭VI7 / / 7^{13} | V 7^{13} / / / / |

B♭:

IIIm7 ♭III7 / / | IIm$^{11}_{7}$ ♭II$^{+11}_{7}$ / / $\|$ CODA   IM7 / / / | ·/. $\|$

D.C. al Coda   Fine

(Medium fast)

(13) $\|:$ IM6 / / / | ·/. / / / | IV7 / / / | ·/. / / / | II7 / / / | IIm7 V7^{9} /

E♭:

1. IIIm7 ♭III°7 / / | IIm7 V7 / / $:\|$ 2. IIm7 #II°7 / / | IM6 / / / / | IM6 / /

G♭:

IIm7 V 7^{13} / | IM6 / / / | IIm7 V 7^{13} / | IM6 / / / | IIm7 V 7^{13} / |

A:

IM6 / / / | V7 / / / / | CODA IIm7 #II°7 / / | IM6 / / / $\|$

E♭: D.C. al Coda

(Fast)

(14) $\|:$ IM7^{9} / / / | ·/. / / | IV 7^{+11}_{13} / / / | ·/. / / | IIm7 / / / | V7 / / / / |

F:

IM6 / / / | ·/. $:\|$ Vm 7 / / / | I7 / / / / | IVM6 / / / | ·/. |

IVm♭7 / / / | ·/. ♭III7^{9} II7^{9} / | IIm7 V7 / $\|$ IM7^{9} / / / | ·/. |

II7^{9} / / / | ·/. IIm7 / / / | V7 / / / / | IM6 / / / | ·/. $\|$

Fine

(Fast)

(15) ‖: IM7 / / / / | ·/. | IV7(13) / / / / | ·/. | ⊕ IM6 / / / / | [1. VIm7 / / / / |
Eb:

| II7 / / / / | V7 / / / / :‖ [2. IIm7 / / V7 / / | IM6 / / / / | ·/. ‖ VIIm7(11) / / / / | III7 / / / / |

| IM7 / / / / | ·/. | IIIø7 / / / / | VI+5(7) / / / / | II7(9) / / / / | V7 / / / / ‖

D. C. al Coda

CODA ⊕ | II7 / / / / | IIm7 / / V7 / / | IM6 / / / / | ·/. ‖

Fine

(Medium fast)

(16) ‖: IM7(9) / / / / | ·/. | IV7(13) / / / / | ·/. | IIm7(9, 11) / / / / | V+5(7) / / / / |
Eb

("B" section)

| IM6(9) / / / / | ·/. :‖ IIm7(9) / / / / | V7(13) / / / / | IM7 / / / / |

Fine Ab:

| ·/. | IIm7(9) / / / / | V7(13) / / / / | IM7 / / / / | bVI7 / / V7 / / ‖

Gb: Eb: *D. C. al Fine*

C. Tunes which start on IV^M7 or IV^M6

(Medium fast)

(17) ‖: IVM7 / / / / | V7(b9) / / / / | IM7(9) / / / / | bIII°7 / / / / | IIm7 / / / / | bIII°7 / / / / | ⊕
F:

| IM6 / / / / | [1. I7 / / / / :‖ [2. IM6 / / / / ‖ IIm7(11) / / / / | V7(9) / / / / |

D:

| IM7 / / / / | ·/. | VIm7 / / / / | II7 / / / / | IIIm7 / / / / | I7 / / / / ‖

F:

D. C. al Coda

CODA ⊕ | IIIm7 / / / / | bIII°7 / / / / | IIm7(9) / / / / | V7(13) / / / / | IM6 / / / / | ·/. ‖

Fine

(Medium)

(18) G:

IVM7 | IVm7 | bVII7 | IM7^9

bIIIm7 | bVI7 | IIm7 | V7 | VII∅7 III7 | VIm6

1. | II7 | IIm7 | Vm7 I7^9 | 2. IIm7^9 V7^{13} | IM6

(Medium slow)

(19) Bb:

IVM7 | IVm♮7 | IM7 | II7^9 | IIm7

V7^{13} | I7 | VII7 | bVII7 VII7 IM6 | I7 | I7 | VII7 bVII7

Fine

VI7 | II7^9 | IIm7 bVI7 | V7

D. C. al Fine

(Slow)

(20) Bb:

IVM7 | IVm6 | IM7 | V+5$^{9}_{7}$

IM6 | 1. VI7 | II7^9

2. IIm7^9 | V7 I7 | III∅7 | VI7 | II7 III7

VIm6 | IVM7 | IVm6 V7^{13} | IM6

D. Tunes whose first four chords are I^M7, VII^ϕ7, III^7, VI^M (temporary modulation to relative minor)

(Slow)

(21) [musical notation]

(Fast)

(22) [musical notation]

(23) Blues progression (e) in Appendix C.

E. Tunes which use $\flat V^{\phi 7}$ or $\flat V^{m7}$ as the first or second chord, usually continuing around the cycle of fifths

(Slow)

(27) D: IM7 | bVø7 VII7 | IIIø7 | VI7 | II7(9) | 1. IIm7 V7 |

IM7 | IIm7 V7 | 2. V+5(7) | IM6 | %. ‖ Im6 | %. |

Fine f#m:

IIø7(b9) | IIø7 V7 | V7 | %. | IIIm7 VI7 | IIm7(11) V7 ‖

D: D.C. al Coda

CODA | IIm7 V7 | IIIm7 | VI7 | II7(9) | V+5(7) | IM6 | %. ‖

Fine

(Medium fast)

(28) Ab: bVø7 IVm7 | IIIm7 bIIIm7 | IIm7 V7(13) | IIIm7 bIIIm7 | bVø7 bIVm7 |

IIIm7 bIIIm7 | IIm7 V7(13) | IM6 | :‖ IIm7 V7 | IM7 VI7 |

("B" section)

Fine Db:

IIm7 V7 | IM7 | IIm7 V7 | IM7 VI7 | IIm7 V7(+11) | IIm7(11) V7 ‖

Eb: Ab: D.C. al Fine

(Slow)

(29) G: bVm7(11) | VII7 | IM7 | %. | Vm7(9) | I7(13) |

IVM7 | IVm7 | IM7(sus.4) ‖ bVø7 | VII7 | IIIm7 |

VI7 | IM7(sus.4) | IIm7 V7 | IIm7(9) | V7 ‖

D: G:

VI+5(7) | %. | IIm7(11)(9) | %. | IVm b7 | %. |

IM7(9) | %. ‖ bVm7 | VII7 | IIø7 |

VI7 | IIø7 | V7(b9) | IM7 | %. ‖

PART II
TUNES HAVING SIMILAR "B" SECTIONS

A. Tunes whose "B" section is the same as the "A" section, except that the "B" section occurs a perfect fourth up from the original key

(Medium)

(30) IM6   IIm7   V$^{+9}_7$ IM7   IIm7   V7   I7
Bb:

IVM7   IVm$\natural$7   IIIm7   bIIIm7   IIm7   bII7   IM6   *Fine*

("B" section)

IM6   IIm7   V$^{+9}_7$ IM7   IIm$^9_7$ V7   I7
Eb:

IVM7   IVm$\natural$7   IIIm7   bIIIm7   IIm7   bII7   IM6   V7
Bb: *D.C. al Fine*

(medium fast)

(31) IM7   IIm7   V$^{13}_7$ IM6   IVm7   bVII7   IM6   VIm7
Bb:

("B" section)

IIm7   V$^{13}_7$ IM6   *Fine*   IM7   IIm7   V$^{13}_7$ IM6
Eb:

IVm7   bVII7   IM6   VIm7   IIm7   V$^{13}_7$ IM6
    D.C. al Fine

(Fast)

(31) IM6   IIm7   V7   IM6   IM6
F:

("B" section)

IIm7   V7   IM6   IM6   IIm7   V7   IM6
Fine   Bb:

("C" section)

IM6   IIm7   V7   IM6   I7   bVII7
    F:

bVI7   V7   I7   bVII7   bVI7   V7
    D.C. al Fine

(Medium)

(32) Im6 | bVI7 V+5(7) | Im6 | ·/. | Im6 | bVI7 V+5(7) |
fm:

Im6 | ·/. ‖ ("B" section) Im6 | bVI7 V+5(7) | Im6 | ·/. |
bbm:

Im6 | bVI7 V+5(7) | Im6 | ·/. ‖ ("C" section) Vm7(9) | I+5(7) |
fm: Fine

IVm7(9) | ·/. | IIm7 | V+5(7) | IM7(9) | IIø7 V7 ‖
         Ab: fm: D.C. al Fine

B. Tunes which modulate up a perfect fourth for the first half of the "B" section, then modulate up another major second (perfect fifth up from original key) in second half of "B" section

(Fast)

(33) ‖: IIm7(9) V7 | IM7(9) | IIm7 V7 | IM6 | IIm7(9) V7 |
Eb:

IIIm7 VI7 | IIm7 V7 | IM6 | ("B" section) IIm7(11) V7(13) | IM7 VI7 |
                                    Ab:

IIm7(11) V7(13) | IM7 | IIm7(11) V7(13) | IM7 VI7 | IIm7(11) V7(13) | V7 ‖
Bb: Eb: D.C. al Coda

CODA | IM6 VI7(9) | IIm7 V7 | IM6 ‖
                                    Fine

(34) See "B" section of (28).

C. Tunes which have successive modulations downward by half-steps in the "B" section

D. Tunes which modulate up a perfect fourth for the first half of the "B" section, then modulate down a major second for the second half

(Slow)

(37) Eb: | IIm7(9) V7 | IM7(9) VIm7 | bVI7 V7 | bVII7 VI7 | II7(13)(+11) | ("B" section)

| IIm7(9) V7 | IM7 | ·/. :‖ Fine Ab: IIm7(9) V7(13) | ·/. |

| IM6 | ·/. Gb: IIm7(9) V7(13) | ·/. | IM6 | IIm7 V+5(7) Eb: ‖ D. C. al Fine

(Medium)

(38) Eb: ‖: IM7(9) | IIm7 V7(13) | IM7(9) | Db: IIm7 V7 | IM6 |

F: | IIø7 V7(b9) | IM7 | Eb: IIø7 V7 | :‖ Ab: ("B" section) IM7 | ·/. |

Gb: | IIm7 V7(13) | IM7 | ·/. | Eb: IIm7 | V7 V+5(7) ‖ D. C. al Coda

CODA | IIIø7 | bVII7 VI7 | IIm7 #II°7 | IM6 ‖ Fine

(Fast)

(39) F: ‖: IM7 | IIm7(11) V7 | ·/. | IM7 | VIm#7 | II7(9) | ("B" section)

| IIm7 V7 | IM7 | :‖ Fine Bb: IIm7 V7(9) | IM7 | IIm7(11) V7 |

| IM7 | IIm7 V7(9) | IM7 | IIm7(11) | Ab: IIm7(11) V7 | F: ‖ D. C. al Fine

(40) See "B" section of (16).

E. Tunes which modulate up a major third for the "B" section and remain there for the duration of the "B" section

(Medium)

IIm7 V7 | IM7 | IIm7 V7 | IM7 |

(44) Ab:

("B" section)

IIm7 V7 | IM7 | IIm7 V7 | IM7 |

C:

V7 | IIm7 V7 | IM7 | IIm7 V7 |

Ab:

IIIø7 | VI7 | IIm7 | VI+5^{7} | IIm7^{11} |

IVm♭7 | IIm7 V7 | IM6 |

(45) see "B" section of (5).

(Fast)

IIm7 V7^{9} | IM7 | IIm7 V7^{9} |

(46) Ab:

IM7 | ("B" section) IIm7 V7^{9} | IM7 |

C:

IIm7 V7^{9} | IM7 | IIm7 V7 |

E:

IM7 VIm7 | IIm7 V7 | IM7 |

Ab:

IIm7 V7^{9} | IM7 | IIIø7 VI+5^{7} IIm7^{9} V7$^{13}_{9}$ |

IIIø7 VI+5^{7} | IIm7^{9} | V7^{9} | IM6 |

F. Tunes which modulate up a major third for the first half of the "B" section, then modulate up a minor third from there for the second half

(Medium fast)

(47)
‖: IM7 / / / / | IIm7 V7 / / | Vm7 I7 / / | IVm7 ♭VII7 / / | IIIm7 ♭IIIm7 / / |
A♭:

IIm7 V$^{13}_9$7 / / | IM6 / / / | ⊕ IIm7 V7 / / | 2. IIm7 V7 / / ‖ ("B" section) IM7 ♭IIm7 / / |
1.   :‖
C:

IIm7 V7 / / | IM7 / / / | IIm7 V7 / / | IM7 ♭IIm7 / / | IIm7 V7 / / |
E♭:

IM7 / / / | IIm7 V7 / / ‖   CODA ⊕ IM6 / / / ‖
A♭: D.C. al Coda   Fine

(Medium fast)

(48)
‖: IM7 / / / | IIm^{9}7 V7 / / | IM7 / / / | IIm^{9}7 V7 / / | Vm^{9}7 I^{13}7 / / |
E♭:

IVM7 IVm7 / / | IM6 / / / | ·/· :‖ ("B" section) IM7 VIm7 / / | IIm7 V^{9}7 / / | IM7 VIm7 / / |
                    Fine G:

IIm7 V^{13}7 / / | IM7 VIm7 / / | IIm7 V7 / / | ♭VI7 / / / | V7 / / / ‖
B♭:   E♭:   D.C. al Fine

(Slow)

(49)
‖: IM7 VIm^{9}7 / / | IV^{9}7 / / / | IM7 VIm^{9}7 / / | IV^{9}7 / / / |
E♭:

IIIm7 ♭IIIm7 / / | IIm7 V7 / / | 1. IM7 VI7 / / | IIm7 V7 / / :‖
                                          ("B" section)

2. IM6 / / / | ·/· ‖ IIm7 V^{11}7 V$^{♭9}$7 / | IM7 VI7 / / | IIm7 V7 / / |
                    Fine G:

IM7 / / / | IIm^{9}7 IIm7 V7 | IM7 VIm7 / / | IIm7 V7 / / | IIIm7 V7 / / ‖
B♭:   E♭: D.C. al Fine

(Medium fast)

(50) IM6 / / / / | IIm7 / V7 / / | IIIm7¹¹ VI7 / / | IIm7 / V7⁹ / | IM6 / / / / |

Eb:

IIm7 / V7 / | IM6 / / / | ·/. :‖ IM7 VIm7 / | IIm7 V7 / |

("B" section)

Fine G:

IM7 / / / | ·/. | IM7 VIm7 / | IIm7 V7 / | IM7 / / / | V7 / / / ‖

Bb: Eb: D.C. al Fine

(Very fast)

(51) ‖: I7 / / / | ·/. | VII7 / / / | ·/. | bVII7 / / / | ·/. | VI7 / / / | ·/. |

Eb:

bVI7 / / / | ·/. | V7 / / / | ·/. | IM7 / / / | ·/. | ·/. | ·/. :‖

Fine

("B" section)

IM7 / / / | bII°7 / / / | IIm7 / / / | V7 / / / | IM7 / / / |

G:

bII°7 / / / | IIm7 / / / | V7 / / / | IM7 / / / | bII°7 / / / |

Bb:

IIm7 / / / | V7 / / / | IM6 / / / | ·/. | IIm7 / / / | V7 / / / ‖

Eb: D.C. al Fine

G. Tunes which modulate up a minor third for the "B" section

(Fast)

(52) IM7 / / / / | ·/. | ·/. | ·/. | Im6 / / / / | ·/. | ·/. | ·/. |
G:

IIm7 / / / / | V7 / / / / | bVII 7 $^{13}_{+11}$ / / / / | VI7 / / / / | IIm7 ^{9} / / / / | V $^{13}_7$ / / / / |

("B" section)

IM7 / / / / | ·/. ‖ IIm7 / / / / | V7 / / / / | IM7 / / / / | VIm7 / / / / |
Fine Bb:

IIm7 / / / / | V7 / / / / | IM7 / / / / | ·/. | IIm7 ^{11} / / / / | V7 ^{9} / / / / |
G:

IM7 ^{9} / / / / | ·/. | IIm7 ^{11} / / / / | V7 / / / / | IM7 / / / / | IIm7 ^{9} V $^{13}_7$ / / / / ‖
E: G: D.C. al Fine

(Very fast)

(53) IM6 / / / / | IIm7 ^{9} V7 / / / / | IM7 / / / / | IIm7 V7 / / / / | IM6 / / / / |
F:

("B" section)

IIm7 V7 ^{9} / / / / | IM6 / / / / | IIm7 ^{9} V7 / / / / | IM6 ‖ / / / / | IIm7 ^{9} V7 / / / / |
Ab:

IM7 / / / / | IIm7 ^{11} V7 / / / / | IM7 / / / / | IIm7 V7 / / / / | IIm7 ^{11} / / / / | V7 / / / / ‖
C: F:

IM6 ‖ / / / / | IIm7 ^{9} V7 / / / / | IM7 / / / / | IIm7 V7 / / / / | IM6 / / / / |

IIm7 V7 ^{9} / / / / | IM6 / / / / | IIm7 ^{9} V7 / / / / ‖ Vm7 / / / / | I7 / / / / |

IVM7 / / / / | IVm♭7 / / / / | IM6 / / / / | IIm7 ^{9} V7 / / / / | IM6 / / / / | ·/. ‖

(Slow)

(54)
$$\text{IIm7}^{9} \quad \text{IIIm7 ♭III7} \quad \text{IIm7} \quad \text{V7}^{9} \quad \text{IM6} \quad \text{IIIm7} \quad \text{VI7}$$
F:

$$\text{IIm7}^{9} \quad \text{IIIm7 ♭III7} \quad \text{IIm7} \quad \text{V7}^{9} \quad \text{Vm7}^{9} \quad \text{I 7}^{13}$$

("B" section)

$$\text{IVM7} \quad \text{IIm7} \quad \text{V7} \quad \text{IM7} \quad \text{IM6}$$
Ab: cm:

$$\text{IIø7} \quad \text{V7} \quad \text{IM7} \quad \text{IIm7} \quad \text{V7} \quad \text{IIIm7}^{9} \quad \text{IIIm7 ♭III7}$$
C: F:

$$\text{IIm7} \quad \text{V7}^{9} \quad \text{IM7} \quad \text{IIm7}^{9} \quad \text{IIø7} \quad \text{V+5}^{7}$$
bbm:

$$\text{Im6} \quad \text{Im6} \quad \text{V+5}^{7} \quad \text{Im6} \quad \text{V+5}^{7} \quad \text{IM7} \quad \text{V+5}^{7}$$
fm: Db:

$$\text{IM7} \quad \text{IIm7}^{9} \quad \text{IIIm7 ♭III7} \quad \text{IIø7} \quad \text{V+5}^{7} \quad \text{Im6}$$
F: fm:

(Very fast)

(55)
$$\text{IM7} \quad \text{II7}$$
F:

$$\text{IVM7} \quad \text{IVm7}^{9} \quad \text{IIm7} \quad \text{V7}^{9}$$

("B" section)

$$\text{IM6} \quad \text{IM7} \quad \text{IIm7} \quad \text{V7} \quad \text{IM6}$$
Ab:

$$\text{IM7} \quad \text{IIm7} \quad \text{V7} \quad \text{IM6} \quad \text{V+5}^{7} \quad \text{IM7}$$
F:

$$\text{♭III°7} \quad \text{IIm7} \quad \text{V 7}^{13} \quad \text{IM6}$$

(Slow)

(56) II∅7 V7 IM7 VI⁷♭9 IIm7 V⁷♭9

C:

1. III∅7 VI⁷♭9 2. IM6 ("B" section) IIm7 V7

E♭:

IM7 ♭IIIm7 ♭VI7 III∅7 VI7

C: D. C. al Coda

CODA III∅7 VI♭⁷5 II∅7 V7 IM6 Fine

(Very fast)

(57) IM7 VI7 IIm7 V7

F: ("B" section)

IM6 IIm7⁹ V7⁹ IM7⁹

Fine A♭:

IIIm7⁹ VI7 IIm7 V+⁷5

F: D. C. al Fine

(Slow)

(58) IM7 VI⁷♭9 IIm7 IVm6 V7

F:

IM6 IIm7 V7⁹ IM6 ♭IIIm7 1. IIm7¹¹ V7

A♭: F:

2. IIm7¹¹ V⁷¹³ IM6 ("B" section) IM7 VIm7 IIm7 V7

Fine A♭:

IIIm7 VI7⁹ IIm7 V7⁹ VIm7¹¹ II7 IIm7¹¹ V+⁷5

F: D. C. al Fine

(59) See "B" section of (13).
(60) See "B" section of (3).

H. Tunes which modulate down a major third for the "B" section

(Slow)

(61) IM7   VI⁷♭⁹   IIm7   V7   IM♭5⁷   Vm7   I7   IVM7   IVm⁷⁹
F:

IIIm7   VI7   IIm7   V⁷¹³   IM7   ('/.   ("B" section) IM7   VIm7   IIIm⁷⁹   V7
Fine   D♭:

IM7   VI7   IIm⁷⁹   V7   IM7   VIm7   IIm⁷¹¹   V+5⁷⁹
F: D.C. al Fine

(Slow)

(62) IM7   ♭IIIm7 ♭VI7   IIm7   III⁷⁺¹¹   VIm7   IIm♯7   IIIm7   VI7
G:

IIm⁷⁹   IVm6   IIIm7   VI7   IIm⁷¹¹   V7   1. '/. : 2. IM6
Fine

IM7   VIm7   IIm7   V7   IIIm7   VI⁷♭⁹   IIm⁷¹¹   V7
E♭:

IM7   VIm7   IIIm6   IIm⁷¹¹   V+5⁷   V⁷¹³
G: D.C. al Fine

(Medium)

(63) IM7 '/. IVm⁷¹¹   ♭VII7   IM7 '/.
C:

VIIm7   III⁷⁹   IIm7   V⁷⁹   ("B" section) IM7 '/.   VIm⁷⁹
A♭:   C:

II7   IIm7   V♭5⁷   IM7   ♭IIIM7   ♭VIM7   ♭IIM♭5⁷

(67) See "B" section of (26).

I. Tunes which modulate to a minor key whose keynote is a major third interval above the original key

(Slow)

(68) IM7 | Vm7 I7 | IVM6 | IVm6 | IM7 VI7 |

Bb:

IIm7 V7 | IM6 | | *Fine* | Im6 ("B" section) | IIø7 V+5 ($^{b9}_{7}$) | Im6 |

dm:

IIø7 V7 | Im6 | IIø7 V+5 ($^{b9}_{7}$) | Im6 | IIm7 V7 ||

Bb: D. C. al Fine

(Medium)

(69) IM7 | | IIm7 (^{11}) | V7 | Vm7 (^{9}) |

Eb:

I7 (^{13}) | IVM7 V7 (^{13}) | IM6 | : Im6 ("B" section) | | IIø7 |

gm:

V7 | Im6 | Im7 VI7 | IIm7 | V7 ||

D. C. al Coda

CODA IIIm7 VI7 | IIm7 V7 | IM6 | | *Fine*

(Fast)

(70) IM6 | IVm7 bVI7 | IM6 | IVm7 bVII7 | IIIm7 VI7 ($^{+9}$) |

Ab:

IIm7 V+5 (^{7}) | IM6 | | *Fine* | Im6 ("B" section) | IIø7 V7 | Im6 |

cm:

IIø7 V7 | Im6 | IIø7 V7 | Im7 VI7 | IIm7 V7 ||

Ab: D. C. al Fine

(Slow)

(71) IM6   VIm7^{11} IIm7^{9} V7 | IM6   VIm7^{11} | II7   V7^{9}

Eb:

Vm7   I7   IVM7   VI7 | 1. II7   IIm7   V7 :|

| 2. II7   V7   IM6 | Im6   IIø7   V7   Im6   ("B" section)

Fine gm:

II7   bII7   IM7   VIm7   IIm7   V7   IIm7   V7

Bb: Eb: D.C. al Fine

(Slow)

(72) IM7   VIm7^{9} IIm7   V7   bVø7   IVM7   IIIm7   VI7   IIm7   VIIø7^{11} III7^{+9}

Bb:

VIm6   IIm7   V7 | 1. 𝄍 :| 2. IM6 | Im6   IIø7   V+5^{7} ("B" section)

Fine dm:

Im6   IIø7   V+5^{7} Im6   VI7   IIm7   V7

Bb: D.C. al Fine

(Fast)

(73) IM6   IVm7   IIIm7   VI7   IIm7^{9} V7

C:

| 1. IIm7^{11} V7 :| 2. IM6   𝄍   Im6   IIø7^{11} V7   ("B" section)

Fine em:

Im6   V+5^{7} Im6   IIø7   V7   II7^{9} IIm7   V7

dm: C: D.C. al Fine

(Slow)

(74) IM7   bIIIm7^{11} IIIm7^{11} VI7   II7$^{+11}_{13}$ V7^{13} IM6   IIm7   V+5^{7}

C:

IIIm7   VI7   IIm7   V7^{b9} IM6   :| Im6   IIø7   V7   ("B" section)

Fine em:

Im6   bII7   IM7   Im6   𝄍   II7^{b9} IIm7   V7

Ab: cm: C: D.C. al Fine

PART III
MISCELLANEOUS CHARACTERISTICS

A. Tunes which modulate up a major third within the "A" section

(Medium)

(75) IIm7 V7 | IM7 VI7 | IIm7 V7 | IM7 | IIm7 V7 |

Eb: G:

IM6 | IIm7 V7 | IM7 ‖ [1.] IM7 | bIII°7 | IIm7 |

Eb:

V7 | IIIm7 | V7b9 | IIm7 | V7 ‖: [2.] IIm6 |

Eb:

VIm6 | IIm6 | IIIm7 VI7 | IIm7 | V7(13) | IM7 | %. ‖

Fine

(Medium)

(76) IIm7(9) | V7(13) | IM6(9) | %. | IIm7 V7 | %. | IIIm7 |

Eb:

[1.] VI7 ‖ IIm7(9) | V7(13) | IM6(9) | %. | IM6 |

G:

IIm7 V7 | IM7 | VI7 ‖: [2.] I7 | IVM7 | IVmb7 |

Eb:

IM7 | VI7(9) | IIm7 | V7(9) | IM6 | %. ‖

Fine

(Medium)

(77)

F:

A:

F:

Fine

(Medium)

(78)

Eb:

G:

Eb:

Fine

B. Tunes which modulate downward in whole steps

(Very fast)

(79)

(Very fast)

(80)

(Medium)

(81)

(Slow)

(82) IIm7^9 V+5^7 IM6^9 ·/.   IIm7^9 V+5^7

G: F:

IM7^9 ·/.   IIm7 | 1. | V7   IM7   ·/.

Eb:

VII 7$^{+11}_{b9}$ ·/.   IIIm7   VI+5^7 | 2. | IV°7   IM7^9

G: C:

II 7$^{13}_{+11}$ bIIIm7   bVI7   IIm7^9 V7^9 IM6   ·/.   Fine

(Very fast)

(83) IM7   ·/.   Vm7^{11} I 7^{13} IVM7^9 ·/.

Bb:

IVm♮7   ·/.   IM6   ·/.   II7^9 ·/.

IIm7   V 7^{13} | 1. | IIm7   V+5^7 | 2. | IM6   ·/.   Fine

IIm7^9 V 7^{13} IM7^9 ·/.   IIm7^9

B: A:

V7^9 IM7   ·/.   IIm7^9 V 7^{13}

G:

IM7^9 ·/.   VIm7^9 II7^9 IIm7   V+5^7

Bb: D. C. al Fine

(84) See (39).

JERRY COKER is a tenor saxophonist and an educator of broad experience. He has developed studio music and jazz programs for Indiana University, Sam Houston State University, the University of Miami and the University of Tennessee, where he is a professor teaching saxophone and jazz. The jazz curriculae he originated are very widely used. He has taught and directed in locations around the world for National Stage Band Camps, Tanglewood Camp of the New England Conservatory, and Jerry Coker Summer Camps.

Also well known as a professional musician, Jerry Coker has been a featured soloist with Stan Kenton, Woody Herman, Clare Fischer, Frank Sinatra, and the Boston Symphony Orchestra. He has made a number of recordings, some of them of his own music. His books, available in several languages, include *Improvising Jazz, The Jazz Idiom, Listening to Jazz, Patterns for Jazz, The Complete Method for Improvisation, Drones for Improvisation,* and *Jazz Keyboard.*